GRANDPA'S ADVENTURES IN THE US NAVY

SOUL SEARCHING ON THE WAY TO MARS

VOLUME II

Jerry Werner

Dedication

To my Grandchildren.

I wrote this book for you. My hope is that my stories and experiences have a positive influence on your life. (Listed in birth order) Zachary "Zach" Werner, Aviya Werner, Lillian "Strudel" Weidmann, Alexander "Nemo" Gregory, and those yet to be born.

Acknowledgment

Editors (alphabetically)

Amazon Direct Publishing

Barbara Werner Cramer

Susan Werner Herr

Matthew Futterman

Jill Werner Johnson

Larry "Vert" Neal

Jan Weidmann

Arlene Werner

Matthew Werner

Michael Werner

Content Contributors (alphabetically)

Minnie Chu

Michael French

Bruce Gallemore

Alan Grube

David Laws

Oliver Linberg, Jr

Hank Turowski

Joani Leach Sheppard

Jemma Futterman Weidmann

Christine McKay Werner

Life Goals Contributors (chronologically)

Parents: John and Betty Werner

Siblings: Tom, Larry, Barb, Kathy, Sharon, and Susan

Uncle: Bob Feyen

Pastor: Father Thomas Crowley

Teachers: Elk Mound School Faculty, with special mention to Mrs. Norma Parker.

High School Classmates: Elk Mound Class of 1966

Professors: US Naval Academy

USNA Classmates: 29th Company Class of 1971

VT-1: LT Mike Grocki

VT-4: LCDR Bob Stoddert

Mentor: CAPT Jack Endacott

Wife: Christine McKay Werner

VF-102: Drex Bradshaw, Bill Denning, Sam Montgomery, Larry Neal, Bill Foster, Mike Matton, and the entire squadron aircraft maintenance department.

Best friends: Mike and Norma French, Larry and Sue Neal

Top Gun: Larry "Vert" Neal

Bethesda Naval Hospital: Dr. William W Simmons

Naval Test Center: Stuart Fitrell and Catholic Chaplain Edward T Hill

Table of Contents

About the Author

Jerry Werner is currently enjoying retirement, splitting his time between two vibrant cities, Manhattan and Montreal and world travel with his wife Arlene. His journey to this point has been quite an adventurous one, filled with diverse experiences.

Following an exciting Navy career, he transitioned into the business world, where he became an executive in the energy conservation industry and applied his problem-solving skills and leadership abilities in more peaceful pursuits.

In addition, he taught college for 20 years as an adjunct professor, and finished his career as the leader of his own business management consulting firm.

It's been a remarkable journey, and he looks forward to new adventures in this next phase of life.

Foreword

Dear Zachary, Aviya, Lilian, Alexander, and yet-to-be-born grandchildren,

As your grandparent, it's an honor to write this book at your parents' request. Within these pages, you'll find the same fireside stories I shared when they were young, filled with wonder and eager to learn about the world. But this book is more than just a collection of stories. It's a time capsule that will take you back to the last century, where you learn about a time now but a memory. Each story is infused with life lessons and advice I've gathered from my experiences and wisdom passed on to me. So, settle in, and let's journey through time together.

I hope you will find as much joy in reading these pages as I did in writing them.

With love,

Grandpa (Also known as Opa)

Dear Valued Readers,

If you like stories of high adventure, where life and death hang in the balance, you've come to the right place. I should've been dead more than a dozen times. If you want to know what it is like to be on an "astronaut track" and how to go from obscurity to NASA's doorstep, this book will give you some clues.

You will be riding along with me as we take a spin in the world's fastest fighter jet. We will not only break the sound barrier together, we will go more than two times the speed of sound and almost die doing it! You will learn what it is like to get shot out of a cannon (aircraft carrier catapult.) We will survive a Category 5 hurricane on a US Navy destroyer. You will share a cell with me in a prisoner-of-war camp. We will experience the joy of being in a coffin filled with garbage. We will share five weeks of adventure at the real Top Gun fighter weapons school. We will meet the Soviet defector who stole the MiG-25. And there will still be some time left over for humor, ghosts and romance.

Here's to the journey!

Jerry "Disco" Werner,

Lieutenant Commander, U.S. Navy (Retired)

Chapter 1
Life and Death in a Navy Fighter Squadron (Continued)

Redemption

Shortly after my "worst night ever" at the aircraft carrier and the chewing out by my Commanding Officer, Dick Wyman, I got a new guy in my backseat, Sam Montgomery. Sam had multiple cruises as an F-4 Phantom RIO. He was not only very experienced, he had a really cool head, and was definitely one of the best RIOs in the Navy. On top of that, he was a fine human being. He flew with me through all of July, August and September. He was not only supremely capable of doing his own job, he had the experience to give me coaching, that was very helpful in many situations. In other words, he made me a better pilot.

Drexel Bradshaw was the man who welcomed me to the squadron, in February, by telling me that he did not need another (effing) nugget. Around July 1st, he became the squadron's new Commanding Officer, beginning his 18 month tenure. He made the decision to put Sam in my back seat. After a few weeks, we all noticed a big improvement in my flying and landings on the carrier.

Late in the summer, Sam and I went up against the Skipper and his RIO in a series of one-on-one dogfights. We won all three! If there was any one occasion that really helped my cause, I believe it was that flight. Bradshaw witnessed how good I was at air combat maneuvering and decided to send me to Top Gun. I had Sam to thank.

Drex "Goober" Bradshaw, addressing the Maintenance Officers and Chief Petty Officers

Looking back on my story, it's clear that positive, supportive decisions were made by many individuals, along the way, that made all the difference. The decision to send me to Top Gun was one of them. Drex did not pick me as the primary pilot to Top Gun, that went to Russ "Craze" Plappert. But he chose me as the alternate and that was good enough for me! He also named me officer-in-charge of the 40-person detachment responsible for maintaining three airplanes during the six week training program. (Two airplanes belonged to us, the third belonged to our sister squadron, VF-33. I was also responsible for maintaining theirs, too.) That assignment looked good on my fitness report, too.

The full story of the Top Gun deployment is found in the Chapter-called The Real Top Gun.

A Real Job in the Maintenance Department

I began with no high value collateral duty in the squadron. They put me in charge of a new system called Personnel Qualifications Standards (PQS), which was a compilation of the minimum knowledge and skills that an individual must demonstrate in order to qualify to stand watches or perform other specific routine duties necessary for the safety, security or proper operation of aircraft or support systems. It was the kind of job that would be handed off to a petty officer rather than a commissioned officer. But I put everything I had into it and got recognized for having the best PQS program in the entire Air Wing.

With my roommate Brian's passing, I was given his job of an Avionics Division Officer. It would qualify as a real job. And it was in the maintenance department, which was valuable for test pilot candidates.

Avionics technicians in VF-102 were responsible for the maintenance and repair of various avionics equipment used on the F-4 Phantom. Some of the equipment they repaired included:

1. Communication Systems: This included radios, transmitters, receivers, and communication antennas used for both air-to-ground and air-to-air communication.

2. Navigation Systems: F-4 Avionics technicians worked on navigation equipment like TACAN, ADF, compass and direct nav.

3. Radar Systems: This involved repair and maintenance of AWG-10 radar system used for target tracking, navigation, and weather detection.

4. Electronic Warfare Systems: Electronic countermeasures and electronic warfare systems that help detect and defend against enemy radar, missiles, or communication systems.

5. Identification Friend or Foe (IFF) Systems: The IFF, now referred to as the transponder, aided in the identification of friendly aircraft through coded signals.

6. Weapons Systems: Certain avionics equipment related to weapon targeting, release systems, or missile guidance.

7. Automatic Carrier Landing System (ACLS): All of the systems required for an automatic landing, auto pilot, auto throttles, and linked communication with the aircraft carrier.

When I took over the Avionics Division, the sailors were pretty depressed. They had just lost their division officer, Brian, and they also had low morale for other reasons. So I did what I always do, Manage By Walking Around (MBWA). This is a technique that works well in any business. It means getting out of your office and seeing, with your own eyes, what your people are doing. I got to know their names, their specialties, their hometowns, and their concerns. I looked over their shoulders to learn how they did their jobs. I asked if they were provided with the right tools whether or not they were getting the cooperation needed from others to get their job done. I asked questions about the challenges they faced. I recognized their birthdays with Kool-Aid and cake. Tim Quinn, my assistant division officer, was also a real asset.

I took action on what I learned, and to the extent that I could influence cooperation from other departments or individuals, I took action there, too.

Then a unique opportunity came along. The Naval Air Test Center needed a squadron to test its newest version of the Automatic Carrier Landing System (ACLS). This system allowed a pilot to fly an approach and "coupled" landing on an aircraft carrier, hands-free.

We pilots, of course, monitored it very closely and were ready to take over if anything went wrong, just like you would if you were sailing down the highway in a Tesla in full autopilot mode. It was strange and a little unsettling, allowing the aircraft to fly and land itself. I felt like I had an invisible robot sitting on my lap, working the stick and throttles.

They chose the VF-102 Diamondbacks to do the testing because we had an excellent maintenance department with the best fighter squadron uptime record. A test center pilot did a large number of automatic landings on the USS Independence and we continued with our squadron pilots doing more coupled landings. Our skipper, Drex Bradshaw, agreed to encourage our guys to try out the system during the daytime so they could have confidence in using it at night. This opportunity arose weeks after my "worst night ever."

In my research, I found some valuable Navy-wide statistics that applied to avionics divisions. Our squadron was doing more ACLS (hands free landings) than anybody else. This was only possible because my avionics division guys were doing their job, keeping the equipment up and running, and the CO was encouraging everybody to use the system. So for the 1977 cruise we became number one in the worldwide US Navy. That really helped morale!

The VF-102 Avionics Division, Best in the US Navy, 1977

Top: Jerry and Tim Quinn. Bottom middle: Sr Chief Greenway

Family Separation

One day, I overheard a Navy chaplain talking about family separation. He said it was the biggest spiritual challenge in the Navy. He was talking about how difficult it is for some people to stay loyal to their spouse, during long separations. And he discussed the challenges a Navy wife faces in handling a household and raising the children, all by herself.

Family separation was also a challenge for those of us who had no children. Six months is a long time to be apart. My wife, Christine, became a middle school math teacher in the Portsmouth school system when we moved to Virginia Beach. She had the summer off, 1977, so she planned to spend a month of it in Europe, the first two weeks with me and the second two weeks with her mother, who was a schoolteacher from Waterbury, CT. We were going to meet in Lucerne, Switzerland. Then plans changed just before the trip. We were still going to meet in Switzerland, but she told me in a letter that her mother was coming along. I was not happy about that, but what could I do?

I was granted two weeks of leave (vacation). I took an overnight train from Naples, Italy, to Lucerne, an 11 hour trip. When I woke up in the morning, we were rolling through the Alps. I had never seen anything so beautiful, snow capped mountains, grand vistas, green meadows, flowers and babbling brooks of crystal clear water, right next to the railroad tracks.

As you may remember, I studied German in school, and I was visiting the part of Switzerland that spoke German. The first words I heard, after getting off the train, were spoken by a young mother pointing to her child, "Nein, nein, nein!" (No, no, no) I smiled.

Christine's flight was landing the next day. She and her mother would be flying on a chartered flight, which was cheaper than regular scheduled airlines. I stayed the night in a very neat little Swiss hotel that we had reserved over the phone. I got breakfast and headed to the airport to meet her. This was a decade before airport security got crazy. I was able to walk right up to the receiving area where the passengers were getting off the plane. I watched all 200 arriving passengers walk past me, but there was no wife and no mother-in-law. I asked an airline worker where they were. She told me that the flight was overbooked, and some people were left behind in New York. I was disappointed and angry, beyond words.

I had bought a bouquet of flowers for Chris. I did not have a bouquet for her mother. I was not pleased that Mildred insisted on tagging along with her daughter on what should've been a reunion with her husband after 4 months. I gave the flowers to a middle-aged woman who looked like she could use them. She responded with "Vielen dank" (thank you very much), and a big smile.

I remind my grandchildren and other young people, in 1977 we did not have Internet, email or text messaging. We didn't even have telephone answering machines. US Mail between the states and the aircraft carrier took about two weeks. In order for me to talk to Chris and find out why she wasn't on the flight, I would have to go to a telephone center that had international calling, and somebody would have to pick up the call on her end.

I returned to the hotel where they directed me to a phone center. I had to pay about three dollars a minute to be connected through an international operator. Nobody picked up my call at the other end. I went back to the telephone center two more times. I finally got through, after three hours, Chris picked up.

What happened? Why weren't they on the airplane? They had arrived late and did not know the flight was overbooked. They were given a coupon for a second flight, but because it was a Chartered flight, it wouldn't leave for another week. Cheaper was not better.

Why did she not call the hotel and let me know she was not on the plane? (It was an eight hour flight.) She could not find the hotel name or phone number.

I got on the train and headed back to Naples so I could return to the ship. I took a bottle of Mateus rose wine with me on the train, but I couldn't enjoy it. It made me sick to my stomach. I was too upset.

We made plans, over the phone, to get together when the ship came into port again, in two weeks. Chris and Mildred met me on the dock. We stayed one night in Naples and then headed to Rome, where we did some sightseeing and stayed two nights.

My mother-in-law was such a pain in the ass, that I was going crazy. The plan was for the three of us to continue north to Germany from Rome, but I couldn't stand traveling with her any longer. She complained about everything, transportation, food, service, accommodations, and people who refused to speak English.

I suggested to Christine that we turn around and go back south to Sorrento, Italy. I had heard many good things about that quaint little town on the Mediterranean, near Naples. We could settle into one hotel for the remaining week of my leave and do day trips from there. She agreed.

We traveled down to Sorrento and ended up having a very nice time. Mildred was a much better travel companion there, and she gave Chris and me free time after dinner, every evening, to do things on our own. The three of us took a day trip to Pompeii, one to the island of Capri and one to Naples. When she returned home and told friends and family about the trip, Mildred said that she had a wonderful time with her son-in-law.

Intercepting Soviet Bombers

Soviet Bomber and VF-102 Phantom

One of the spy vs. spy rituals that occurred regularly between the US and the Soviet Union was overflights of our aircraft carrier task force by their big bombers. Their objective, I assumed, was to take photos and listen to electronic emissions to learn if anything changed with our aircraft, antenna, weapons or the carrier itself.

Our fighter mission was to intercept them, far away from the aircraft carrier, and escort them until they passed out of our area. That also meant positioning our aircraft, in between the bomber and the aircraft carrier, so their photographs included our Phantom in the picture.

When relations between our two countries were warm, we would sometimes see men show up at the windows of the bomber, smile and wave. They would even show us the centerfold from the latest issue of Playboy Magazine, presumably to make us envious that they got it before we did.

When the relations between the two countries were cold, the same man at the window might show us his middle finger. The pilot of the big Soviet bomber (usually a Badger or Bear) might dip a wing in an attempt to crunch a fighter. I'm not sure how that would work in his favor, as he would sustain damage, too. The point being, our adversaries' behavior was quite different, depending on the political relations between the two countries.

Finally, these intercepts were successful 100% of the time because we had good spies in place inside the Soviet Union. They let us know the day before the bomber was coming, its tail number, what Air Force Base it was launching from, time of departure, and estimated time overhead of the aircraft carrier. This made it easy to be prepared to intercept them. It also helped avoid triggering World War III by accident.

Soviet Defector and MiG-25 Thief

My last non-flying job at VF-102 was as an aviation fighter strategy and tactics expert. I was sent to a top-secret US Air Force school. I learned the latest information about our enemies, particularly the Soviet Union. I was among a small group of aviators at NAS Oceana, who were invited to meet the Soviet defector, Viktor Belenko.

In 1976, at the height of the Cold War, Viktor Belenko made one of the most daring defections in aviation history by piloting a top-secret Soviet MiG-25 Foxbat fighter jet to Japan, an ally of the United States.

It was during this time that Belenko began doubting the Soviet system and its ideological foundations. He grew disillusioned with the regime and became increasingly aware of the limitations imposed upon Soviet citizens, particularly the constant surveillance and control by the state.

Belenko also felt that the MiG-25, while an impressive aircraft, had its technological flaws that were concealed from the world. Wanting to reveal the aircraft's shortcomings and escape from the Soviet Union, he began planning his defection.

On September 6, 1976, Belenko executed his audacious plan. He took off from Chuguyevka near Vladivostok in his MiG-25 and, without authorization, flew east towards Japan. His daring escape went undetected for some time due to the Foxbat's immense speed, which made it difficult for Soviet radar to track him.

After a 400-mile flight, Belenko landed his MiG-25 at Hakodate airport in Hokkaido, Japan. His defection caused a major international sensation and provided the U.S., along with its allies, an unprecedented opportunity to examine the advanced Soviet aircraft. (The aircraft that he stole is shown in the photo below. You can see that he ran off the end of the runway.)

The United States, Japan, and other Western countries thoroughly analyzed the MiG-25, exposing its weaknesses and technological limitations. This intelligence coup significantly helped U.S. military planning and defense strategies during the Cold War.

It also encouraged the Soviets to do their own spying. While I was stationed in NAS Oceana, I was told that a Soviet spy gained access to the hangar where I worked. It was also where the new F-14 Tomcats were parked. I assumed that he took high quality, close-up photographs of the aircraft and absconded with classified printed materials. The Navy immediately erected a fence around the hangar, with video cameras, and controlled entry, which did not exist before. But the horse had already bolted from the stables.

Meanwhile, Belenko settled in the United States and began sharing his insights and knowledge about Soviet aviation with the U.S. military. He went on to earn U.S. citizenship and became a respected consultant specializing in aerospace technology and defense issues.

It is worth noting that Belenko's family, like other Soviet citizens, experienced the effects of living under a repressive regime. Soviet society was characterized by pervasive government surveillance, limited freedom of speech, and strict control over citizens' lives. Defecting or having family members who defected was seen as an act of treason against the state, and often resulted in severe consequences for the individuals left behind.

I was intrigued with the opportunity to meet Belenko. He was introduced to us by his handler and interpreter, in 1979. He spoke some English and used an American fighter pilot term early in the interview which brought a big laugh from the small audience. He used the term "shit hot" which means something that's really cool. But after using the term three more times in the next 20 minutes, it was clear that his command of English was limited and his understanding of his audience even more so.

Belenko lived in the Soviet Union at a time when their economy was in the tank. People waited for hours in line for basic food items. The first time he was taken to a grocery store in the USA, he thought it was the same propaganda ploy used by the Soviet Union to impress foreign visitors. They would stock a single store with shelves full of food stuff. But when he was given the freedom to travel alone, he discovered that all of our grocery stores were stocked with abundance. He told us that we lived in a land of plenty and he was grateful that he could share in it.

He said that the poor economy affected the Soviet Air Force as well. They had so little aviation fuel that their pilots were lucky to fly two hours a month. We American fighter pilots complained that we could not be combat ready if we flew less than 20 hours a month. It was another sign that the Soviet Union was in rapid decline.

I came away from the interview with mixed feelings. When I arrived, I thought he was a hero to the West. But when I left, I thought he was a traitor to his country who stole one of its prize possessions and left a wife and son behind to fend for themselves. It's not fair of me to judge him because I was never in his shoes. But it's also not clear to me that he was a hero.

How Did You Get Your Navy Call Sign?

With the popular movie sequel Top Gun: Maverick, in theaters at the time of this writing, friends and family asked me to critique the movie. I did so and included it in the Chapter called The

Real Top Gun. Some had another question, "What was your call sign and how did you get it?" This short story explains.

First, it should be clear that no new fighter pilot chooses his or her own nickname or call sign. Just like Native Americans, the tribe assigns the name after they get to know the youngster. They choose a name that gives us insight into their personality.

Native Americans named their children complimentary names such as Running Bear or Lily of the Valley. A Navy fighter squadron tribe, on the other hand, assigns names to its young fighter aircrew that are rarely complimentary. Here are some examples:

Sam Montgomery had a skin condition on his back. His call sign became "Fungus." On his department head tour, he became "SAM," based on his initials. It was later changed to "Skates," when Sam, as a new Skipper, was found rollerblading on the flight deck.

Drex Bradshaw was born and raised in Suffolk, VA, The Peanut Capital of the World. His call sign became "Goober," another word for peanut.

On his first trip ashore, Jon Everett drank too much, got sick on the whale boat ride back to the aircraft carrier and threw up on a senior officer. His call sign became "Ralphie."

Stu Benner loved to eat beans. When he did, his farts would clear out the entire ready room. His call sign became "Beanie."

Bill Denning had oversized pointed ears. His call sign, as a junior officer, became "Elf." He changed it to "Snake," when he became the Skipper of the Diamondbacks.

Knowing all of this, I was apprehensive about what name they would give me. I learned that if you angrily protested the assigned name, it was much more likely to stick. So when they came up with my call sign, I was relieved, but couldn't let on. I put on a good show and protested loudly.

Now that it is no longer classified, I can reveal my call sign, but I first want to give you a little background. My squadron mates were aware that I was a disc jockey at the Naval Academy and on the aircraft carrier radio station. I always brought a boombox with me and played music at squadron parties. My wife Chris and I taught junior officers and their wives how to disco dance. So it makes sense that my call sign became "DISCO." (Sam Montgomery first announced the name in the USS Independence News, after our successful missile shoot together.)

"Disco" turned out to be a great call sign during the heat of battle when people were yelling over radio static and pilots struggled with G-forces just to get the words out. "Disco" always came through loud and clear!

"Disco, you have a bogey, right 3 o'clock high!"

"Tally Ho! Engaging!"

Sam "SAM" Montgomery and Jerry "Disco" Werner

On the occasion of Sam's 500th carrier landing

Note to grandchildren:

I think most of the lessons in this chapter are self evident, but let's go over them for reinforcement.

My welcome to the VF-102 Diamondbacks left a lot to be desired, but before the year was up, it had all turned around. Drex Bradshaw, who turned out to be a great leader, went from

"I don't want you."

to

"I'm sending you to Top Gun!"

I believe the main reason I got the nod to Top Gun was because Sam Montgomery flew with me for three months in a row and provided a strong endorsement. With seasoned coaching and encouragement, he helped refine the gold in the nugget.

Worst Night Ever (Last chapter, Volume I): There is an expression in the Navy, "It was his turn in the barrel." They said that about me when I needed five passes to get aboard the aircraft carrier. Everybody eventually has a really bad day or night. You will, too. But remember, no matter how bad things look, "This too shall pass."

When should you ask for help from a Higher Power? Remember, I failed the underwater swim 200 times before I asked for help. In Volume 1, Chapter 14, I made four unsuccessful passes at the aircraft carrier. Should I have asked for help sooner? If we start thinking that we do everything, all by ourselves, Nature has a way of correcting that misconception.

Family Separation: All human relationships need good planning and communication, especially in a marriage. The trip to meet my wife in Lucerne, Switzerland, was an example of a failure of both. Fortunately, we salvaged the vacation. So can you, if you're willing to forgive one another.

Chapter 2

Heroes

I was in the Navy for 15 years, spanning the war with Vietnam and the Cold War with the Soviet Union. During a shooting war, fighter pilots were heroes for shooting down enemy airplanes. During the Cold War and peace time, fighter pilots were heroes for saving airplanes and lives.

In my opinion, everyone I flew with was a hero. To strap yourself into a Navy aircraft was an act of courage. You were putting your life at risk in service to your country and your loved ones, every time. According to Tom Wolfe, in his book, *The Right Stuff*, "...the Navy would compile statistics showing that for a career Navy pilot, i.e., one who intended to keep flying for twenty years... there was a 23 percent probability that he would die in an aircraft accident. This did not even include combat deaths, since the military did not classify death in combat as accidental."

In my 9 years flying jets for the U.S. Navy, I lost 31 squadron mates, including three roommates, to aircraft accidents.

Here's an example of heroics. One dark and stormy night, our Skipper, Commander Drex "Goober" Bradshaw, ran into the VF-102 ready room where a dozen of us junior officers were sitting, and shouted,

"Who wants to go out and rescue Louie? He has a total electrical failure?"

Every hand went up!

Why is this significant? Because a night rescue mission in bad weather is very challenging and scary… Your buddy could be running low on fuel. You have to hustle! Put on all of your gear, run up to the flight deck, strap into an airplane, run through all the checks, and get blasted off into that black night!

Then you have to find your buddy. Air traffic control already has him on their radar and they guide you to him so you can do a controlled rendezvous. It helps if your own radar is working. If he truly has a *total* electric failure, he will not have any lights. If it's a moonless night, it can be very difficult to join up safely and lead him back.

Once you find him, you fly up next to him. Using hand signals, ask how much fuel they have left. If they have the right amount of fuel to land on the aircraft carrier, that's where you go. You do all the radio communication for them. Then you lead them around to the back of the boat and down the glidepath, with him flying formation on your wing. When you get to the point where they are set up to land themselves, you peel off. You land your airplane once they are safely on board.

If they don't have the optimal amount of fuel to land on the aircraft carrier, they may exercise other options, such as flying around in circles to burn off excess fuel, fly to the "bingo" airport, or eject near the aircraft carrier to be rescued from the water. (Dumping fuel is not an option with an electrical failure.)

From the perspective of the pilot flying an airplane at night, with a total electric failure, is a serious emergency, especially when you are out to sea and have no ground references. You're entirely in the dark, no lights inside or outside of the airplane. The pilot has to fly the airplane with a red lens flashlight, clipped to his survival vest, shining on the very basic instruments remaining: altimeter, vertical speed indicator, airspeed, angle of attack, turn needle and wet compass. Very stressful!

How did the Skipper know that Lou Figari had a total electrical failure? Because air traffic control radar spotted him flying in a special triangular pattern that tells the controller that he is experiencing a total electric failure and cannot communicate by radio.

In summary, I considered everybody in VF-102 to be heroes. They willingly put themselves at personal risk in order to save their friends. The Skipper chose another crew that night to save Louie and his RIO, and those guys did a great job and brought everybody home safely!

Let's go back to the concept of "heroes" saving airplanes in peacetime. I had the opportunity and got credit for saving four airplanes. These incidents eventually helped build my résumé for my application to Test Pilot School. All occurred while with the VF-102 Diamondbacks, flying the F-4J Phantom.

1. We Lost What?!, See Chapter 7.

2. On a Melting Wing and a Prayer

April 16, 1977 in Tail Number 157297 with Jim "Harry" Reasoner, my Radar Intercept Officer (RIO), we launched off the USS Independence (CV-62) for a daytime flight. During the mission, I got a warning light indicating that we had lost our utility hydraulic system. I described the incident in a letter to my parents, written on April 23, 1977.

"Flying is going fine. I did have an unusual emergency the other day. I lost the utility hydraulic system. There are two backup systems and a hot bleed air duct at 650°F burst open and started melting the right wing. However, I used the emergency air system to blow down my landing gear and flaps and brought it in for a perfect landing. I got to be 'Hero-for-a-day.' The airplane hasn't flown since. It's awaiting a new right wing."

VF-102 air crew disembarking from a Phantom after flight, 1977

I am sure my parents didn't really understand everything I was talking about, but they knew that "hero-for-a-day" was a good thing. In order for you to understand what happened, I need to explain three systems that were involved.

The first is the *utility hydraulic system.* It provides the means to raise and lower the landing gear and the wing flaps so one can land aboard an aircraft carrier. It is also required for operation of the nose gear steering and wheel brakes, after you land.

The second is the *bleed air system.* It provides 650°F compressed air from the jet engines to power a number of things including cabin heating, air conditioning, cockpit pressurization, and smooth air over the wings during landing (called boundary layer control air).

The third is a backup, the *compressed air system*. It has a separate tank, filled with high-pressure air, attached to the actuators of each of the wheels and the wing flaps. During an emergency, such as this, it provides a means to "blow down" the landing gear and the wing flaps, so the pilot can land on a carrier.

When I got the Utility Hydraulic Failure warning light, I immediately reduced power and looked for secondary indications. Then the Bleed Air Failure warning light flashed on. I switched off the bleed air system. I looked for any evidence of fire and saw none.

I talked it over with my RIO and he ran through the emergency checklist. I notified the Air Boss that we had an emergency and needed to return to land immediately. Harry ran through the checklist again, making sure we didn't miss anything. As it turns out, we did miss one thing. We had to go to the back of the book to find out how to handle the lack of boundary layer air over the wings during landing. He told me that the checklist prescribed flying a flatter angle of attack (AOA), 17 instead of 19, on the AOA meter.

We blew down the landing gear and the wing flaps, at a safe altitude, made sure the wheels were all down and locked and the airplane was controllable. We then made our approach to landing at the flatter, faster angle of attack. I must have handled it well because my landing was graded perfect ("OK 3 wire") by the Landing Signal Officer.

Normally, after an arrested landing, you raise your hook and taxi very quickly out of the landing area to make room for the next airplane about to land. But because we had no brakes or nose gear steering, we had to stay put with our hook still held by the arresting cable until they connected our airplane to a tow bar and pulled us to a parking spot.

Upon inspection, they found that the whole emergency was caused by a hole in the bleed air duct in the starboard/right wing. The blast of very hot air burned through and ruptured a hydraulic line. It then started to melt the wing.

Heroes? We got kudos for how we "nuggets" (rookies) handled the emergency. The bleed air leak was causing damage to the right wing that could have resulted in a catastrophic loss of the airplane. We saved it by quick thinking, prompt action and following the emergency procedures.

Could my teammates have handled the same situation successfully? Yes, I'm sure most of them could have. I just happened to be in the "right" place at the right time…

3. Skidding off the runway at 100 mph

It was a rainy day in Virginia Beach, October 28, 1977. I was in Tail Number 157281. We had just returned from our Mediterranean cruise and were back home at Naval Air Station (NAS) Oceana, Virginia Beach, VA. Larry "Vert" Neal was my RIO in my backseat. We had just recently been paired up and were told that we would be going to Top Gun together as a crew. We were really excited about that!

We had completed our day's mission, which was practicing intercepts with teammates over the Atlantic Ocean and we were returning to base. We had to do an instrument approach, as it was cloudy and rainy all the way down. We did a TACAN instrument approach and we were cleared to land on runway 05L. (TACAN is described in another chapter.)

I did the normal F-4 approach at 145 knots (167 MPH), with wing flaps full down for the slowest approach. When we touched down, I pulled the throttles back to idle, deployed the drogue chute, applied the wheel brakes and waited until we slowed below 100 knots (115 mph) to activate the nose wheel steering.

As soon as I pressed the button to engage nose wheel steering, it made a hard right turn! I reacted immediately and pressed the power steering disconnect switch, but it would not release. I pressed it several more times. The nose wheels continued tugging us urgently to the right.

OH, CRAP!

I countered with hard braking on the left rudder pedal, but with standing water on the runway, braking wasn't sufficient. It felt like we could hydroplane or blow a tire and make the situation worse.

"Tower, 103, steering failure! We're leaving the runway!" I transmitted on Tower frequency.

As we left the runway, at around 100 mph, I shut down both engines to keep them from sucking up any debris and controlled the airplane with braking, as best I could. We bumped along and plowed through grass, sod, and mud for about 150 feet before we came to a sudden stop. We were still upright. Yay!

Larry and I climbed out of the airplane to assess the damage. All we saw was mud and grass on the tires. Everything else looked OK. Yay, again!

We were soon met with emergency vehicles and flashing lights.

They gave us a ride back to the hangar, and we went to the ready room to debrief with our Commanding Officer (CO), CDR Drex Bradshaw and the Safety Officer. I told my story. The CO believed me, but the Safety Officer appeared skeptical. (He was not a pilot and that can make a difference in perspective.) He did not like me and gave me the impression that he would like to stick me with something, if he could. Some people are like that.

We returned the next day to learn that the maintenance department found no damage to the airplane (good news), but they were not able to duplicate the problem with the nose wheel steering (bad news). The standard term used on maintenance paperwork is "Unable to duplicate on deck." It happened quite often with the F-4. Mechanical equipment that failed, when subjected to changes in atmospheric pressure, was hard to duplicate at sea level. Also problems that occurred while under g-forces, sometimes disappeared at 1g.

The Safety Officer was grinning like the Cheshire cat. He told me that maintenance was unable to find any problem with the nose wheel steering and that he would have to write me up for pilot error. That would probably mean the end of my hopes of ever getting into test pilot school or the astronaut program.

I went to the aircraft maintenance department head, Lieutenant Commander Mike Matton. Mike was very smart and a true professional. He was someone I expected to be an admiral one day. I explained the situation to Mike and we went to the hangar floor.

There on the hangar floor was my airplane up on a hoist, similar to your car in the shop with all the wheels up off the floor. He asked the chief petty officer in charge of the repair to connect the electric power and external hydraulics and have his tech sit in the pilot's seat and switch on nose wheel steering. He did so and everything worked as advertised. The wheels turned left and the wheels turned right. No problems. It was just as they had reported.

LCDR Matton then directed the chief to bring him a bucket of water. With the system still powered up, he took the bucket of water and dumped it on the nose wheel steering actuator, just above the tires. The nose wheel immediately yanked to the right!

"WHAP!!" …… (Proving that I was right!)

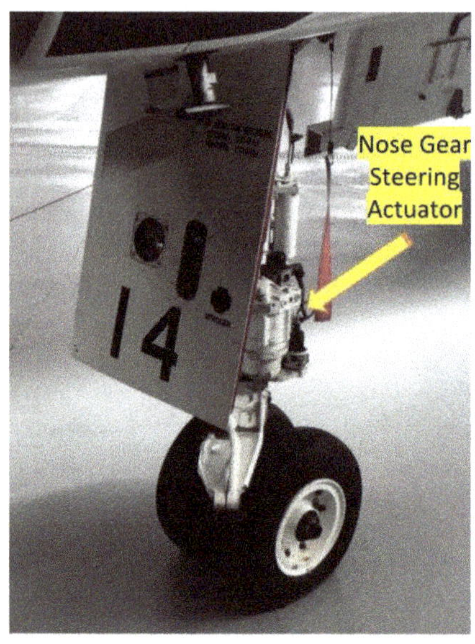

Relieved, I thanked Mike, the Chief and his crew.

The Safety officer slithered off, looking dejected…

Was I a hero for saving this airplane? The safety officer said, "No." But the CO said, "Yes." Why? Because many airplanes that left the runway - over time - were significantly damaged. Some resulted in fatalities. This one had no ill effects. He was happy with that outcome.

4. Landing with a Broken Tail

This incident occurred in Spring, 1979. I don't remember who is in my backseat as my Radar Intercept Officer (RIO). We embarked on two exciting flights that day, participating in the rare scenario called, "One vs. Many." One vs. Many means every man for himself. Everybody is the enemy. (All fighter pilots were men at that time.) It was a chance to be in the air with dozens of other fighter aircraft, all of them trying to shoot you down. Or to look at it from the positive side, a target rich environment!

The F-4 Phantom was among the fastest of the bunch. We knew we would have to stay fast and use that advantage. Back then we had a saying, "Speed is life!" (We did not say, "I feel the need for speed!" That was invented by the writers of the first Top Gun movie, 1986.)

Both flights were in our usual military operating area over the Atlantic Ocean off the coast of North Carolina, W-72. We had to stay beyond 35 miles from shore, because we would be going supersonic and sonic booms are not permitted near civilization. The morning flight was a disappointment. We didn't even see another airplane. Our radar was not working, so my RIO was unable to find any bandits. The good news was we did not get shot down. The bad news was we did not get any "kills."

The afternoon flight was also One vs. Many. While the morning flight was only Navy and Marine Corps aircraft, the afternoon flight included US Air Force F-15s. Our plan was to climb to 40,000 feet, go very fast, and look for targets of opportunity underneath us. When we got to the southern border of the operating area, we would reverse course, swoop down and fly just above sea level so all of the bandits would be above us.

As planned, we climbed to 40,000 feet and accelerated to Mach 1.3 (~1000 mph). We closely scanned the area beneath us, but again without radar, we did not see any other airplanes. Disappointing. When I got to the southern border of the operating area, I rolled inverted, pulled the power back to idle, and descended rapidly down towards the wave tops. I maintained supersonic air speed downhill and we were doing about Mach 1.2 when I leveled off at 500 feet above the ocean, heading in the opposite direction. I slid the throttles up to full power to maintain our speed.

That's when it happened. I heard/felt a very loud noise.

"**POW**!" The air frame shuddered! — I shuddered! —- It felt like we had hit something or somebody!

I pulled the power back and popped up to 5000 feet. The airplane was still flying OK. Then I asked my RIO to call on the radio and request assistance from one of our VF-102 Diamondback friends who were in the area. We gave them our location and one crew came over quickly in their F-4 to check us out.

They immediately saw the problem. They told us that we had lost half of our horizontal stabilizer on the tail of the airplane. (It's called a "stabilator" on the F-4) It provides the aerodynamic leverage to climb and descend. This loss would definitely affect my ability to land the plane safely.

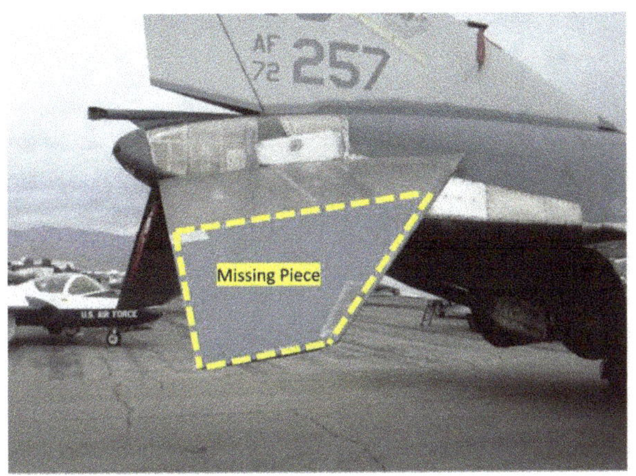

F-4 Phantom Stabilator, depicting where the section was missing

As any good pilot would do, I tested the airplane's controllability at a safe altitude in the landing configuration. I put the landing gear and flaps down and simulated an approach to landing at 5000 feet altitude, over the ocean, at the normal approach speed, but that was not fast enough. I could not maintain the proper rate of descent. I increased the speed, in increments, until I reached 180 knots (207 mph), where the aircraft felt quite stable and controllable. That would be my approach speed.

We called our commanding officer on the radio. We discussed the situation with him, and he agreed that I should do the approach at 180 knots. We declared an emergency and air traffic control cleared the airspace for us so we could make a straight in approach to NAS Oceana Runway 05R. It took more than 30 minutes to get there. Our teammates stuck with us, flying formation on my wing the entire way.

As the airport came into sight, it looked like a circus. The admiral's car was there with its blue flags flying. There were multiple emergency vehicles with flashing lights, and the local TV station WTKR was also there with their truck and cameras! I guess they were all anticipating a newsworthy show.

"Sorry, guys, if you're looking for drama, I'm going to disappoint you!" I said to my RIO.

180 knots turned out to be the right speed. I greased it on, like a good airline pilot, to the cheering of my comrades and the dismay of the press!

Yippee!!

Postscript:

I was not a hero for making this landing, even though some airplanes were lost due to similar problems. Any good F-4 Phantom pilot could've done it (even an Air Force pilot!). I think I got credit because of the public visibility, senior officers and TV presence. Most of the Navy's mistakes and mishaps are away from home, out to sea, invisible to the public.

We lost a big chunk of the tail because of high speed aerodynamic pressures. I did not exceed any speed limits or g-limits. The section had been weakened by saltwater corrosion and fatigue. All Navy F-4s were temporarily grounded until each of them was inspected. A couple of others in our squadron showed similar signs of corrosion. They were repaired.

The pictures below show the problem with taking complex, expensive machines out to sea. Normal saltwater spray itself is an issue, but storms at sea can be a much more serious problem, sometimes immersing entire aircraft in saltwater!

USS Independence (CV-62) Atlantic Crossing, March 1977

Advice to my Grandchildren:

1. Keep your expensive machines away from saltwater

2. Keep track of your special accomplishments. Put them in a folder. You never know when they'll come in handy if nothing more than cheering you up someday!

Chapter 3

Moments of Stark Terror

WHAT did you really see?

"They're going to hit us!" he screams from the front seat.

Who is screaming in a Navy jet? What does he see that I don't see? Are we going to die?

This chapter was inspired by a Navy transport pilot, who described his job as "endless hours of boredom interspersed with moments of stark terror." In all my years of flying navy jets, I don't remember being bored, but I did have some pretty scary moments that really got my attention. I describe five of those in this chapter.

After getting my Navy Wings of Gold, I was assigned to a training squadron, VT-9 at the Naval Air Station (NAS), Meridian, MS, instead of a fighter squadron. That was a disappointing 2–3-year career setback. I would have to be the best Basic Jet flight Instructor at VT-9 to have another chance at fighters. I was eager to prove myself with my first student. It was August, 1974.

Lieutenant Jerry Werner, Flight Instructor,

VT-9 NAS Meridian, standing next to the Basic Jet Trainer,

the T-2B Buckeye

Basic Jet Flight Instruction included six phases: Aircraft Familiarization, Basic Instruments, Precision Aerobatics, Formation, Night Flying, and Radio Instruments. I was assigned as my first student's primary instructor for the first phase, Aircraft Familiarization.

My first student wore a non-standard leather name tag on his flight suit that simply read "Earl." It had a piece of masking tape covering the Navy Wings at the top of the patch. I had worn something similar the week before I got my wings. So as soon as I qualified, I could just rip the masking tape off and expose my new wings. But he was many months away from getting his wings, if ever. I probably should've questioned it, but I didn't. Instead, I called him Earl.

Earl did not turn out to be a very good student. On our first flight, he dumped our fuel on the way to the training area. We had to return immediately to land. What possessed him to go out of his way in the cockpit to find and pull the fuel dump handle? I will never know. My gut told me that I should have given him a failing grade on that first flight, but I did not. He was my first student. It was our first flight.

He managed to do one knucklehead thing or another, on almost every flight. When I told these tales to my wife, Christine, a naval officer and school teacher, she said it sounded like I was spoon feeding him. She recommended that I give him a down. (A failing grade)

I never gave him a down. Another instructor had to do it for me. He failed Earl on his first phase check flight, Aircraft Familiarization. I was embarrassed. I felt like I had failed, instead of him.

That takes us back up to the top of the page. Two months later, October 19, 1974, Earl and I were wrapping up our 15th training flight together. He was flying in the front seat of a T-2B. The sun had set and it was getting quite dark as we entered the NAS Meridian airport flight pattern from the south to circle around to land on Runway 19.

Then I hear a bloodcurdling scream from the front seat,

"They're going to hit us!"

I grabbed the controls,

"I've got the aircraft!" I said.

I felt a chill go up my spine. I quickly scanned the area in front of us. I saw nothing.

"Well," I thought, "If they're going to hit us, we're dead. I don't see a thing."

I asked, "Earl, what did you see?"

"My name is not Earl, it's Neal!"

WTF?

He just screamed that we're about to die and now he's more concerned with what name I call him. He has a name tag that reads "Earl" and he has responded to "Earl" for eight weeks. Unbelievable!

I did not give control of the airplane back to him, instead I landed and taxied back to the flight line. We went inside to debrief.

The next day, I asked the Operations Officer to reassign Neal to another instructor.

"I've gone as far as I can with this guy. It's time for someone else to take over."

Postscript:

What did he see that made him scream? I believe he saw two airplanes coming into the break facing us. Two TA-4 Skyhawks flying formations entered the landing pattern from the north and split up in front of us. He may have seen the lights from the two aircraft separate from one another quickly, making it appear as if a single airplane was about to hit us. That's my theory.

What about the name tag? When asked, Neal said he was wearing his uncle's name tag in honor of him. His uncle Earl, a naval aviator, was killed in action. Why did he not correct me earlier and tell me that his name was not Earl, but Neal? Who knows.

This story does not have a happy ending. After handing him off to other instructors, Neal washed out of Pilot Training and was invited to join the Naval Flight Officer Training Program. He passed that course and became a Bombardier/Navigator (non-pilot) in an A-6 Intruder squadron. But he and his pilot flew into the water one night in the Mediterranean. Like his uncle Earl, Neal died in service to his country. May his soul rest in peace.

Neal was one of the 31 squadron mates that I lost to aircraft accidents.

Footnote:

Why did I choose to tell this story, where it wasn't even a near miss? Because, in over 50 years of flying, it is the only time I've ever heard a pilot emit a scream of any kind. It was so unexpected that it struck me with terror!!

Professional pilots are pretty disciplined human beings. The US Air Force even has a saying:

"Shut up and die like a pilot!"

The most you are likely to hear from any pilot who is about to die is:

"We're going down."

Advice to my grandchildren:

When you are new on the job and you feel pressure to do the right thing, trust your gut, it's more reliable than your brain.

If you become a pilot, maintain your sense of priorities. Always be prepared for the unexpected.

In your role as a parent, teacher, or coach, keep in mind that some people have an aptitude for what you're trying to teach them and some do not.

Night Fright

How does one fly into the water at night? I'll tell you how I almost did, March 22, 1978. My buddy and favorite RIO, Larry "Vert" Neal, saved me.

We were flying practice intercepts with our squadron mates over the Atlantic Ocean, off the coast of North Carolina. We were with the VF-102 Diamondbacks station at NAS Oceana, Virginia. Larry and I were flying F-4J Phantom tail number 157298.

Our job that night was to intercept two F-4s, flown by our squadron buddies, who were playing the role of bad guys ("bandits"). We played the role of bogey (unknown aircraft). We needed to shoot them down with missiles before they reached the beach. (Simulated)

Larry and I liked to play the role of wily bogey, as in crafty and cunning. On this run, we decided to approach them from high to low. We started out above 25,000 feet. On a dark night, a pilot can't see the horizon or the water, so the lowest I wanted to fly over the open ocean was 5000 feet, our agreed-upon "hard deck" or "platform." So I set the radar altimeter to warn us if we got too low.

The intercept training exercise began with about 60 miles of separation from the "enemy" airplanes. Larry had some difficulty finding them on the radar. The mode in the F-4's AWG-10 radar designed to find a target when looking down, from high to low, is "Pulse Doppler." But Pulse Doppler hardly ever worked in the F-4 and it was not working that night. So Larry had to use the "Pulse" mode, which required tricky workarounds involving side lobes and receiver gain.

Once he found the bandits on his radar screen, it looked like a single target, not two airplanes. We discussed that they might be playing wily bandit. Perhaps they were flying very close together to make it look like a single target. Then they could surprise us by splitting up and attacking us as a team. We had a closure rate of about 900 knots. (1000+ mph)

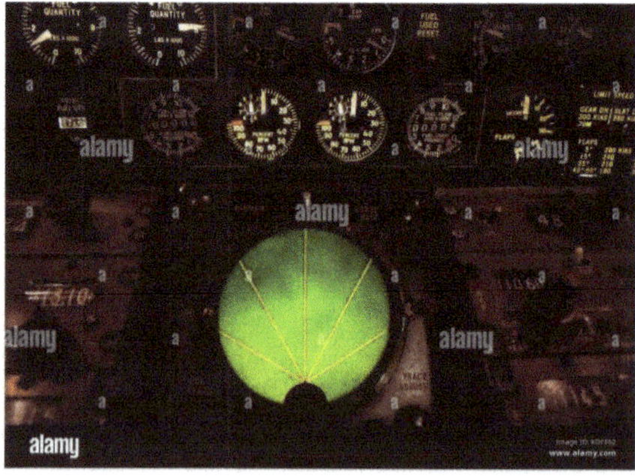

Fighter Aircraft Radar Scope

Instead of doing my job, flying the airplane, I got too involved in Larry's job, finding and interpreting the targets on the radar.

All of a sudden, Vert comes up on the intercom and says abruptly,

"Disco, PLATFORM!"

(Interpretation: We just busted through our hard deck!)

Jesus Christ! I pulled up immediately and added power and felt significant G forces on my butt.

The altimeter momentarily dipped BELOW SEA LEVEL! Holy shit!

How did I allow that? How did I bust our minimums? That means that we were a few seconds away from hitting the water… Lord, have mercy!

The altitude-hold feature of the autopilot did not hold after I engaged it at 5000 feet, and I did not notice it. And for some reason, the radar altimeter did not do its job of getting my attention, either. Thank God Larry did his job. Otherwise, neither one of us would be here today to tell the story

Postscript:

A contributing factor may have been a lack of sleep from the night before, but that's no excuse.

Advice to my grandchildren:

Do your own job and let your professional partner do his/hers…And be ready to back up your buddy if they fall "asleep."

Death by Firing Squad

One of my goals was to accumulate at least 1500 flight hours, so I could qualify to get into the US Naval Test Pilot School, to stay on track to become an astronaut. Another goal was to visit all 50 US states, by planes, trains or automobiles. The two goals went hand-in-hand.

While an instructor at VT-9 in Meridian, Mississippi, I flew about one cross-country flight per month, to build up my hours. On one trip, my Naval Academy classmate and copilot, Bob Brubaker, joined me. I cannot find the flight in my logbook, but I will never forget what happened. (Log books were maintained by humans and subject to error and omission.) It was 1975. I looked forward to the flight with him because he was a good guy and had a good sense of humor.

Our flight plan to the west coast included stops at McConnell Air Force Base in Kansas and Offutt Air Force Base in Nebraska, two states in which I had never set foot and I could check off my list. We would be flying the T-2C Buckeye twin-engine Navy training jet.

The T-2B/C Buckeye, Basic Jet Trainer

Our flight from Meridian, Mississippi to McConnell Air Force Base in Topeka, Kansas was uneventful.

One of the reasons we liked to land at Air Force bases was because they had better facilities and we got much better customer service than at Navy bases. I was told that was because the Air Force knew how to build new airports the right way. They first built all the facilities, the hangars, ready rooms, bachelor officers' quarters, officer's club, etc. When they ran out of money, they went back to Congress and said, "Hey, we need more money to build a runway!" Congress gave them the money to build a runway. The Navy, they told me, did it backwards. They built the runway first, ran out of money, and then had to beg for enough funds to build decent facilities. They never got enough. I don't know if that story was true, but it looked like it was.

For example, when we got to McConnell, they had free box lunches for aircrew members. I never saw that at any Navy base. They also had a microwave in the pilot lounge. They called it a Radarange, in honor of the technician who discovered microwave cooking while working on a radar system. We are told that it melted a chocolate bar in his pocket. We would not see a microwave at a Navy base for another five years. I did not get a microwave for my family until nine years later.

While I was checking the weather and filing our flight plan for our next destination, Bob was picking up the box lunches for us. He got three boxes of fried chicken. He said they didn't know how many crewmembers we had on a T-2, so they let him take three boxes. They actually had never heard of a T-2.

Bob loved to eat. He was a little overweight for a pilot, but underweight for an American civilian. He started eating one of the box lunches before we left.

We completed our preflight checks, copied and read back our clearance from air traffic control. I taxied to the runway, took off, and climbed to our cruise altitude of 40,000 feet. On the way up there, we encountered some pretty rough turbulence between 25,000 and 35,000 feet. Once we settled in at our cruise altitude, I was doing the flying, and Bob was doing the eating. It was nice and smooth at 40,000 feet.

I don't know if you will find the following airborne conversation humorous or not, but I do. After flying for 50 years and talking to air traffic controllers, the communication is always very disciplined, standard, and boring. Thanks to Bob, this conversation was memorable.

On our way to Offutt Air Force Base, we heard a lot of chatter between air traffic control (Kansas City Center) and commercial airline pilots. They were complaining about the rough air turbulence they were experiencing. United Airlines asked the controller if there was a better altitude. Bob spoke up to the controller and said,

"Kansas City Center, Navy 909, you can tell United that we're eating chicken up here at 40,000 feet!"

The air traffic controller responded,

"Thanks Navy, I will let them know."

"United, we have a Navy crew who says they're eating chicken up at 40,000 feet!"

United Airlines responds,

"Great, please thank Navy. Can you clear us to climb to a chicken eating flight level?"

"Roger, United, maintain current heading, climb to and maintain flight level 410." (41,000 feet)

I laughed my ass off!

Shortly after this conversation, it was time for us to begin our descent. These two Air Force bases, McConnell and Offutt were not very far apart, only about an hour's flight for us.

On the radio, we were passed off from Kansas City Center to Omaha approach control. Then when we got within 20 miles from the airport, we were handed off to Offutt Tower. We requested clearance to land.

It was clear from their response that Offutt's own controllers did not know who we were. They had not been notified of our flight plan. They asked us to do a 360-degree turn until they sorted it out. We did one turn in holding. I noticed that this airfield had a bunch of big bombers, parked on the ramp, the size of B-52s. But I didn't think anything of it. They asked us three times who we were, where we came from, type of aircraft, how many souls on board, etc. They had never heard of a Navy T-2 Buckeye.

Finally Offutt tower cleared us to land on RWY 31. About halfway down the runway, we had slowed enough that they cleared us to turn left and taxi to the ramp. Tower told us to stay on their frequency and did not hand us off to ground control. After taxiing a couple hundred feet onto the flightline, we were told to stop, and shut down.

The path of approach, landing and taxi to encounter with security guards at blue burst.

A vehicle came racing up to us, but it wasn't the typical "Follow Me" truck, it was a military vehicle. Out jumped four guys in fatigues with assault weapons. Two guys raced around to the left side and two guys ran around to the right side. **We were surrounded. I had two weapons pointed at my head. Bob had two weapons pointed at his head.**

US Air Force Guard with weapon

I had seen plenty of guns and violence on TV and movies, but it's different when it's real life and it's your head in the crosshairs. It is terrifying. Why are they doing this? Do they have their safeties on? Do any of them have an itchy trigger finger? If so, we could be dead, instantly.

I called Tower on the radio:

"Tower, Navy 909, what's going on?"

"909, Tower, we are still looking for your flight plan."

"Can you ask them to lower their weapons? Trust me, we are all on the same team."

In what seemed like forever, but was probably less than a minute, they lowered their weapons. We exhaled.

"Tower, 909, can you call McConnell Air Force Base tower by landline and ask for them to confirm our departure from there?"

A few minutes later, Tower came up on the radio:

"Navy, 909, Tower, we found your flight plan. Please exit the aircraft. They will give you a ride into reception."

Security forces packed up and returned to their station. Regular Air Force men gave us a ride into the terminal.

Postscript:

Why didn't they have our flight plan? I don't know. Clearly, we would not have been allowed to take off from McConnell, Air Force Base, without our flight plan being in the "system." That FAA system, as I understood it, was a teletype that printed out the flight plan at each air traffic control location, including the final destination. It's possible there was a problem with Offutt's teletype, or the guy who was responsible for pulling the paper off the machine and giving it to the Tower controllers, did not do his job. Regardless, they were not expecting us.

Why was it such a big deal that they would bring out the guns and threaten to shoot us? Offutt Air Force Base was the US Air Force Strategic Air Command (SAC) headquarters. That meant, not only did they have a bunch of Air Force generals there, but they had a lot of big bombers and nuclear weapons, too. And they had never seen a Navy T-2 Buckeye. As far as they could tell, we were the enemy disguised as a US Navy jet.

When we went inside, they asked me why we were landing at Offutt Air Force Base. I did not tell them that I was checking Nebraska off my US State's list. I told them that we needed fuel.

Advice to my grandchildren:

Even when you have done nothing wrong, you can sometimes find yourself in a tough situation (gun to your head). It's best to stay cool and believe that The Universe/God is looking out for your best interests. And then, exhale…

The Penetration Checklist

Every type of aircraft has a checklist to complete before you descend from cruise altitude down to landing. It is known as a Descent Checklist or Penetration Checklist. Penetration, refers to penetrating clouds and weather. The F-4J Phantom Penetration Checklist had 13 items for the pilot and 7 for the RIO.

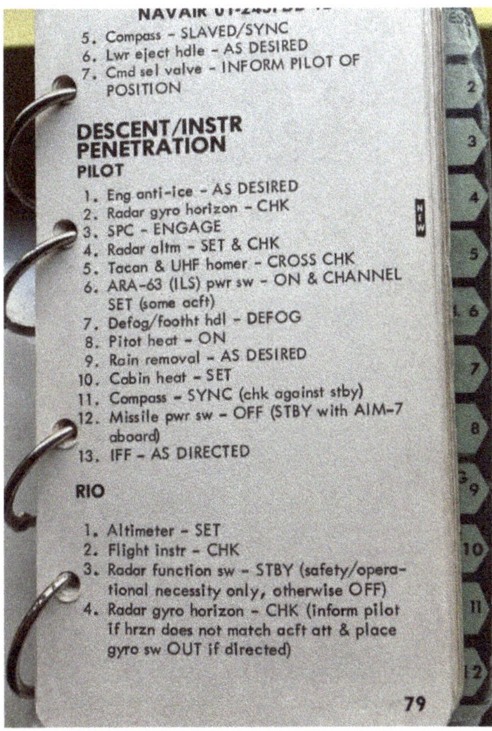

F-4J Phantom Penetration Checklist

One of the most important items on any descent checklist is heating up the windshield. (Pilot #7. DEFOG) Temperatures at high cruise altitudes are usually well below freezing, so when landing at a warm, humid airport, a very cold windscreen can get fogged over, preventing the pilot from seeing the runway to land.

It won't surprise you that young Navy men turned the Penetration Checklist into something sexual. And while the items could vary by individual, two required items on 'An Officer and a

Gentleman's Penetration Checklist' were consent and condom. When Navy pilots heard their buddy was going out on a date, they would sometimes say, "Don't forget your penetration checklist!"

On Friday night, May 12, 1978, I was flying with my favorite RIO, Larry "Vert" Neal, in F-4J Phantom tail number 155767. We were on a 2 1/2 hour leg from an Air Force Base out west (not named Offutt) to the Naval Air Station at Pensacola, Florida. In planning our flight, our weather briefer said Pensacola's forecast was not good enough for Visual Flight Rules (VFR), so we had to choose an alternate destination airport, in case we couldn't land at Pensacola. It had to meet certain weather criteria. We chose Eglin Air Force Base, only about 42 miles from Pensacola. It met the weather conditions for an alternate airport.

About an hour and a half into our flight, Larry called the air traffic controller to check the weather at Pensacola. It had deteriorated badly and was right at cloud ceiling minimums for the type of instrument approach we would be doing. Eglin Air Force Base was still OK as an alternate.

Just before pushing over, from 35,000 feet for our approach to Pensacola, Larry checked again on the weather. Eglin Air Force Base had also deteriorated and was no longer an acceptable alternate airport. While on our descent, Larry asked the controller to find the nearest military airfield that had acceptable weather. That turned out to be 250 miles behind us in Alexandria, Louisiana, England Air Force Base.

It was dark, it was bad weather, and I was busy flying the airplane. I did not follow the entire conversation between Larry and air traffic control. I thought that Eglin Air Force Base, the closest one, was still a good alternative. It was during our descent that Larry cleared up my confusion with the two Air Force Base names that sounded the same. Now, if we missed our approach to Pensacola, we'd have to fly to England Air Force Base, which was 276 miles west of Pensacola. Did we have enough fuel to get there? Larry did not think so. He would have to do the calculations.

So what were we going to do if we could not land in Pensacola? We were between a rock and a hard place. There were no good alternatives. We decided to make the approach and see just how bad the weather was in Pensacola. If we could not land, we'd have to make a decision what to do next. It was very tense. We reviewed our weather minimums for our approach to Runway 7L, one more time: Cloud ceiling had to be at least 500 feet and required minimum visibility was ¾ mile. When air traffic control switched us over to Pensacola Tower, we asked for the actual current weather. He said the ceiling was 400 feet and visibility was 1 mile. We decided to press on.

During my approach to Pensacola, we went right down to minimums. I saw the runway just as we descended below 500 feet. I wasn't thinking about it, but this was the same runway where I landed on top of another aircraft five years earlier. Our approach speed was 145 knots (167 mph). I didn't land on anybody this time.

But, after we touched down and were rolling out, **my windscreen fogged up completely! I couldn't see a thing!**

While attempting to steer straight ahead and stay on the runway, at 100 mph, I opened my canopy. I hung my head out the side into the wind, World War I style, except that I had no white scarf waving in the breeze. I kept us on the runway until we stopped at the end. I taxied into the ramp, again with my head hanging out one side or the other, so I could see where we're going.

VF-102 F-4J Phantom, with both cockpit canopies open

Postscript:

Why did my windshield fog up? You guessed it. In all the last minute confusion over Eglin and England weather, Larry and I both forgot to do the Penetration Checklist.

Did I damage the canopy by opening it at 100 miles an hour? The answer is NO. I checked it out by cycling it several times and everything was OK…. Whew!

But, if it's a choice between losing a canopy and losing an airplane, it is an easy decision. I will always choose to lose the canopy.

Advice to my grandchildren:

1. If you become an instrument rated pilot and your forecast weather at your destination requires an alternate airport, choose an alternate far enough away that it will not be in the same weather system.

2. Whether you're a pilot or not, don't get distracted and forget to do your Penetration Checklist.

Guantanamo Bay, Jake and a Live Missile Shoot

Guantánamo Bay, Cuba

I have never met a Jake that I liked. And the Jake in this story will give me agita twice in the same day. But I am getting ahead of myself.

I was chosen to be the Airwing 7 event project manager for a live missile shoot, the last month I was with the VF-102 Diamondbacks. That was not my actual title, but it was the job. I was responsible for overseeing the planning and coordination that would hopefully result in 10 fighter crews from the two F-4 squadrons, successfully firing live AIM-9 Sidewinder heat-seeking missiles at a drone. The pilots were scheduled to fly into Guantánamo Bay Cuba on Sunday and Monday, and participate in the missile shoot Monday afternoon. Jake, from our sister squadron VF-33, was one of those pilots.

I arrived in GITMO Friday morning so I would have time to meet with the team and prepare for Monday's missile shoot. It was May, 1979. It was many years before GITMO would become famous for housing 911 terrorist suspects.

Guantánamo Bay is the oldest continuously operating US foreign base. It has been leased from the Cuban government since 1903. It is on the eastern end of the island, which is desert-like and has no source of water since its pipeline was cut off by Fidel Castro in 1964. So the US base is supplied by desalination plants that convert seawater to drinking water. That means no washing cars, no watering lawns and no wasting water. Everyone is encouraged to shower together. (I made up that last one…)

If you've been following my story, in earlier chapters, you learned that I was a disc jockey at the Naval Academy radio station and did some DJ stints on a couple of ships where I was stationed, including the aircraft carrier USS Independence. I enjoyed radio stations and playing music for people. That is how I got my fighter pilot call sign, "Disco."

I noticed on Saturday that there was an Armed Forces radio station on the base, Radio GTMO. I stopped by to ask if the Sunday morning DJ might want to sleep in. As it turns out, he did. So I volunteered to take his shift. He gave me a quick check out of the equipment and the keys to the station.

I arrived at the radio station early Sunday morning. When I turned on the lights, I saw what I thought was a big orange mouse race across the floor. Turns out it was not a mouse. It was the biggest cockroach I had ever seen! When I looked for him, I found not one, but two! They didn't bother me too much, as long as they stayed in their corner.

I turned on the equipment and went on the air. I found no good sources for news, weather, or sports, so I mostly played my favorite music, pop songs from the 60's and 70's, including disco, of course! My audience was the roughly 8500 people who lived on the naval base. They were primarily service members and their families. I announced the phone number for the radio station request line. I got a few calls and if I could find the song they requested, I played it for them.

In between records, I was talking about the weather, and saying that it looked like it was going to be another nice sunny day with a high of 80. Most of the callers seemed pleased to have a cheerful voice on Sunday morning radio, but one annoyed lady called in and demanded,

"Why are you giving weather reports? The weather is always the same in GITMO!"

When my shift ended, my relief arrived and so did an attractive young woman, sandy blonde hair, medium height, nice shape, wearing lipstick. She said she wanted to meet the new DJ and tell him that she enjoyed the show. That was the first time that had ever happened to me! (I was accustomed to all male audiences.) I thanked her for coming by and told her that I was only there for the day. I wished her well and I was on my way. I would have invited her to lunch, if I were single.

I enjoyed some of that sunny weather. I reviewed the planning for the missile shoot. I went to happy hour at the Officers Club and had a few rum 'n cokes, with my friends.

Jake

Conversation turned to a new pilot in our sister squadron, VF-33, named Jake. Jake was cool. Jake was funny. Jake was quite the character. He had convinced his audience that he could smash a drinking glass on a bar, chew the glass shards, and swallow them without any harm to him.

I asked, "What's the trick?"

"There is no trick. He really does it. He really chews and swallows glass."

Two other guys chimed in that they had witnessed it as well. They agreed that there was no trick. He was really eating glass. I did not argue with them, but I knew there had to be an illusion involved. And it could be a fairly easy one to do, surrounded by a gang of drunks in a noisy bar! All you need is your own edible glass. Never mind…

"Our Commanding Officer really loves Jake!"

I said good night and went to bed early in the Bachelor Officers Quarters (BOQ). The air was very warm and dry. The BOQ had no air conditioning, but it did have screens on the windows and circulating fans. It was OK for sleeping.

I slept through the night and was awakened before dawn, by a nightmare. A nightmare that a fighter jet was about to land on top of me.

But wait, it was not a nightmare, it was the real thing!!

The most obnoxiously loud screaming jet engine roar I'd ever heard. The whole building was shaking!

I leapt out of bed. I dove underneath!

(Now, if an aircraft really did land on top of me, I don't know what good it would do to be underneath a bed. But in a moment of terror, that is where I went.)

F-4 Phantom very low, with afterburners ignited

The sound faded away. I was beyond Wideawake! I got dressed and went down for breakfast.

In the BOQ breakfast area, everybody was talking about the jet that almost landed on us. Somebody said its afterburners damaged the roof. One of the guys from VF-33 said the pilot was Jake. Jake, the glass eater, had warned them that there would be early reveille for everybody on Monday morning.

The normal landing pattern does not go over the top of the BOQ. Jake had to alter his path significantly and be hundreds of feet too low to be at rooftop level. It was the kind of maneuver, if intentional, that would result in disciplinary action, possibly the loss of one's Wings.

His squadronmates surmised that Jake would come up with a good cover story, and say that he just made a bad approach and had to wave off and go around. Their Skipper loved the guy, so he would want to believe a cover story.

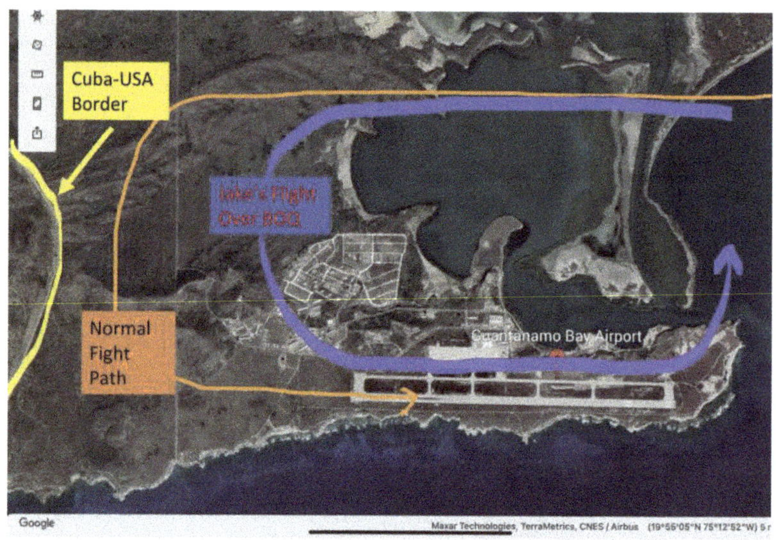

NAS Guantanamo Bay, Cuba

I want to point out that the border between Cuba and the USA is very close to the normal flight path when landing on Runway 10. We were constantly reminded to keep the flight pattern tight so that we did not overfly Cuba. The Cubans would have the right to shoot at us if we did. The risks related to the close border were pointed out in the 1993 movie, *A Few Good Men*. The movie stars

Jack Nicholson, Demi Moore and Tom Cruise. The most memorable line of the movie:

"You can't handle the truth!"

So, when questioned about his bad approach, Jake could have said that he was unfamiliar with the airport and wanted to make sure that he did not overfly Cuba. I don't know what he told his boss. I am also not aware of any retribution to Jake, as a result of that stunt.

Live Missile Shoot

Navy personnel gave me a ride out to the missile test range facility. I did all of the necessary communication, coordination, and planning. At least 100 people were involved, including everybody in the squadrons that prepare the airplanes with missiles and Range personnel, making sure that everything is safe in the air, on the ground and in the water.

Back in the GITMO ready room, a senior officer briefed all of the crews on the plan, safety procedures, and the importance of sparing the one drone that we had available.

VF-102 Diamondbacks F-4J Phantoms, 1977

The plan called for ten F-4 Phantoms, one at a time, each firing a single AIM-9L Sidewinder heat seeking missile at a single drone. (We called it a drone, but it was actually a Remotely Piloted Vehicle or RPV) They would each have to wait their turn, stacked in holding, the Phantoms on one side of the operating area and the drone about 25 miles from them, on the other.

AIM-9L Sidewinder

Navy Remotely Piloted Vehicle (Drone)

When cleared to begin, one F-4 Phantom proceeds in the direction of the drone. After he acquires visual contact, confirms the right distance, and arms the missile. When he hears the growling Sidewinder tone in the pilot's headset, the pilot pulls the trigger and calls out "Fox 2!"

When hearing the words, "Fox 2!," the pilot of the RPV turns the drone very hard and reduces engine power (reduces heat), so that the heat-seeking missile flies right by and does not destroy the drone. With the RPV still intact, the next fighter aircraft can approach and practice its live missile firing. We only had one drone to play with that day, and its value was in the hundreds of thousands of dollars.

The first two Phantom pilots followed the procedure, calling out "Fox 2" so the RPV pilot was alerted to make a hard turn and save the drone.

The third pilot on the list of 10, was Jake. This guy did not follow procedures. When he got the drone in his sights, he pulled the trigger and fired a Sidewinder missile without saying a word to anybody. No "Fox 2." No warning to the drone pilot.

What we heard, instead, was loud cheering over the radio,

"I assholed it! I assholed the son of a bitch!"

The drone was destroyed. It was the end of the missile shoot. If I could have reached his throat, I would've choked him. I'm not the only one who wanted to. Seven F-4 crews could not complete their missile shoot that day because Jake was not a team player.

It was up to his boss, the VF-33 Commanding Officer, to discipline him, but my understanding is that never happened. The Skipper was still fascinated by Jake's ability to eat glass.

Postscript:

I have been very hard on the writers of the two Top Gun movies. I said they were very unrealistic, and that the Navy would never accept the undisciplined behavior exhibited by Tom Cruise's character, Maverick. Maybe I was wrong. Maybe he could get away with more than I thought…

Advice to my grandchildren:

Don't be a Jake, be a team player, please.

Chapter 4

The Defense Department regrets to inform you…

Quote from the first Top Gun movie, by Goose (Anthony Edwards): "The Defense Department regrets to inform you that your sons are dead because they were stupid."

A Very Near Miss

Aircraft near misses are in the news, as I am writing this chapter, March 2023. Here in New York City at JFK, two airplanes came within 1000 feet of each other, because one commercial airliner, without clearance, crossed an active runway and almost got hit by an aircraft taking off. Now, of course, that is very dangerous and needs to be investigated and prevented. But the short story I'm about to tell you is about a near miss, a lot closer than 1000 feet!

I was flying with VF-102 out of our homebase, NAS Oceana, Virginia. I was the lead of a two airplane section. We briefed the flight, manned up our airplanes, and both taxied out together.

I took off first. I thought I heard the tower clear our teammates for takeoff, right after us. I flew out towards our operating area, where we were going to rendezvous. All traffic follows the same southerly flight corridor down the coast (see blue path on chart) and out to the operating area, off the coast of North Carolina. Everybody went out at the same altitude, 15,000 feet, and came back at another altitude, with all traffic flowing over the same visual landmark. The landmark is indicated below as a red bolt of lightning.

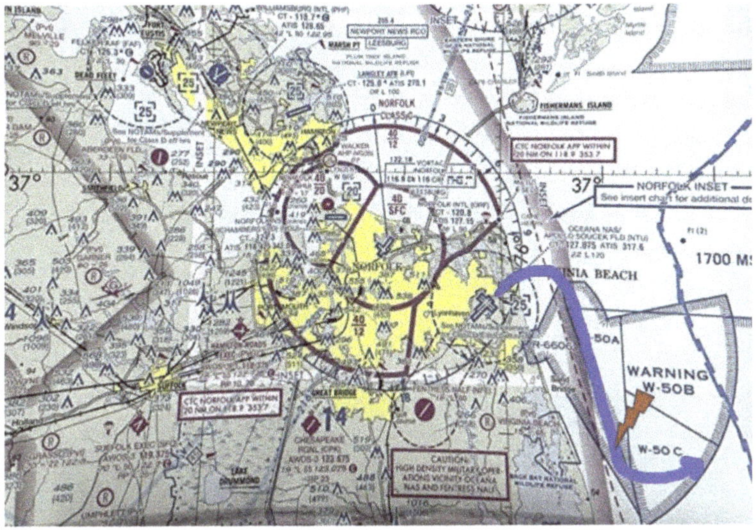

Air Navigation Chart of the Virginia Beach Area

Instead of continuing out to the operating area, where our teammates could join up with us safely, I decided to do a 360° turn at the landmark, thinking that we would meet them there more easily. I completed one turn, and saw nobody. My Radar Intercept Officer (RIO) gave them a call on the radio and asked where they were. No response.

I continued another 360° turn. If the first turn was a big mistake, the second turn was a nearly disastrous blunder! Halfway through the turn what should flash in my windscreen but an A-6 Intruder, so BIG I could see the whites of their eyes right through their tinted visors!! We passed within inches, at a closure rate of 1000 miles an hour! The bow wave air THUMP was enough to tip my wings over! Holy Crap that was close! Heart-in-your-throat-close!

"I am a knucklehead!"

The A-6 Intruder

Postscript:

I don't think I have to explain to anyone how stupid it was to do a flat 360° turn right at the same altitude over the same landmark at which everybody was flying out of Oceana. The only reason I'm here to write about it, is because it wasn't my day to die.

What happened to our teammates who had been cleared for takeoff? They had a mechanical problem, declined to take off, and taxied back to the hangar. It is no excuse, but I did not see or hear the A-6 preparing for or getting cleared for takeoff.

To illustrate how close I thought we came to hitting one another, after we shut down on the ground, I walked around to my wing tip to see if there was any paint on it from the other aircraft! (There was none)

This incident never got reported. I don't remember who my Radar Intercept Officer (RIO) was that day, but I know it wasn't Larry "Vert" Neal. If it were Vert, he would have spoken up and said,

"This is NOT a good idea, Disco!"

Advice to my grandchildren: Don't do a 360 in the middle of a busy highway!

Flameout at 41,000 feet

This is not a story about how close I came to ending my life. This is a story about how close I came to ending my career by doing something stupid.

It was at least my third flight between Mississippi and the West Coast. I was an instructor, assigned to training squadron VT-9 at NAS Meridian, teaching students how to fly their first jet, the T-2C Buckeye.

Jerry Werner next to a T-2C Buckeye, Basic Jet Trainer, 1974

In order to be competitive for entry into the US Naval Test Pilot School, I understood that I would need at least 1500 flight hours. So I flew every extra flight I could. I volunteered for the flights that no one else wanted, such as night flights and spin training. With the agreement and support of my wife, I flew a long cross country training flight, about one weekend a month, frequently to the west coast.

On Sunday, December 28, 1974 I was flying a rare solo cross-country flight. For some reason I couldn't find anyone to take a trip with me that weekend. I was returning home from NAS Alameda, California, where I was visiting my Naval academy roommate Steve Wohler and his wife Linda. We went to Napa Valley wine country. That was back when wine tasting was still free. It was a fun weekend.

I was flying the newest version of the Navy's basic jet trainer, the T-2C Buckeye, Tail Number 158533, call sign Buckeye 303. Its best gas mileage cruising was above 40,000 feet. I stopped for fuel at Nellis Air Force Base, near Las Vegas. Continuing my trip eastward, I was cleared by air traffic control to climb to 41,000 feet, or in their language, Flight Level 410.

The weather was as good as it gets. At 41,000 feet it was clear for 100 miles in every direction. Not a cloud in the sky. We used to jokingly call that weather condition, "severe clear!"

I was looking forward to doing some sightseeing, though it is not normal to do sightseeing from 41,000 feet (8 miles high). Everything usually looks like an ant colony. But in a stretch between

Las Vegas and Albuquerque, there's a lot to be seen from high altitude. The Grand Canyon is so gigantic that it looks absolutely gorgeous from that altitude when the sky is as clear as it was that day. It made me wish that they hadn't made rules against flying down in the canyon itself. I would've liked to have done so, but I was still a kid!

The Grand Canyon

The next featured attraction is the painted desert of New Mexico and Arizona. Vast, colorful and amazingly beautiful.

Arizona Painted Desert

And lastly, on the list of sightseeing attractions, are the meteor impact craters that make portions of the New Mexico and the Arizona desert look like the moon. Incredible!

A New Mexico Meteor Crater (approximately 1 mile in diameter)

But, this chapter's drama is focused on the crossing of a remote desert navigational site called Gallup VORTAC.

The VOR in VORTAC is an abbreviation for Very High Frequency Omni-Directional Range. It is a ground-based electronic system that provides azimuth (direction) information for high and low altitude routes and airport approaches.

The TAC in VORTAC is an abbreviation for TACAN or tactical air navigation system. In addition to directional information, it provides distance measurement called DME.

A VORTAC provides both direction and distance for navigation. It was the primary means of navigation in the 1970s, before inertial navigation and GPS, used today, along with VORTAC.)

My flight plan called for navigating over the Gallup VORTAC, in northwestern New Mexico. I had flown this stretch a few times before and wondered what the Gallup VORTAC looked like, because it was out in the middle of nowhere and I had never seen it. (A VORTAC station looks like an inverted white ice cream cone.)

VORTAC station

As I crossed over the Gallup VORTAC, this time, my curiosity got the best of me. I decided to take a peek. How could there be a VORTAC out here, all by itself, in the middle of nowhere? So I tipped the airplane up on a wing — just for a moment —

I took a look and this is what I saw...

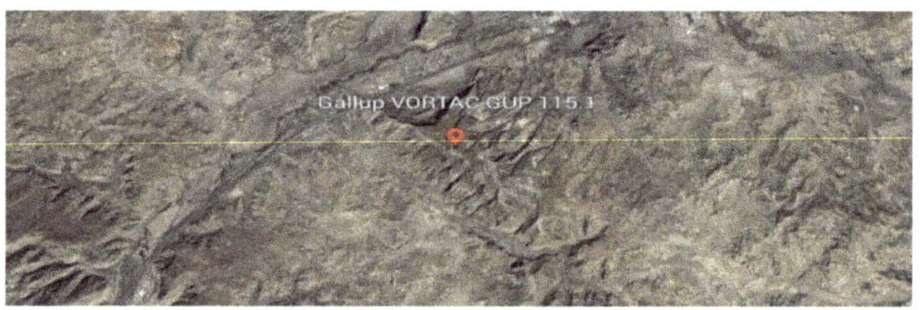

Gallup VORTAC (red symbol) on Google Earth

And then what happened?

Both engines flamed out! ...Z-Z-Z-Z-Z-z-z-z......

ARE YOU KIDDING ME??!!

I knew these new J85-GE-4 engines were touchy at high altitude, but I didn't know they were that touchy! My tipping the aircraft up on a wing disrupted the smooth airflow to the engines and they quit. I knew from my emergency procedures that I would have to descend below 25,000 feet to do an air restart.

"Albuquerque Center, Buckeye 303, I've just lost both my engines. Request descent below 25,000 to restart."

"Buckeye 303, Albuquerque Center, I understand you've lost both engines. Maintain current heading. You are cleared to descend, as required. Please keep me advised."

"Wilco" (Shorthand for "Will comply.")

As any pilot can attest, losing all of your propulsion while airborne creates a tense situation. But I had the advantage of being at a high altitude with plenty of time to think about it and make a plan. I set up a gradual controlled rate of descent. The mind started racing.

"Why did I do that? That was DUMB!"

"I am losing cabin pressurization. Will my blood boil at this altitude? I don't think so."

"I don't have to worry about lack of oxygen because I am wearing an oxygen mask."

"There is no heater without the engines running. It's going to get cold pretty fast. The outside air temperature is -56°F. It's late December, over high desert."

"What do I do if the engines don't restart? I don't see a flat, easy place to land. I see rocks, hills and uneven sandy areas. The Emergency checklist calls for ejecting at 7,000 feet above the ground, if you don't have a suitable airport at which to land. The desert below me is about 7,500 feet above sea level, so if I am going to eject, I need to do it at 14,500 on my altimeter. But I do not plan to eject from the airplane unless it's a last resort."

"I have practiced engine out landings. I do see a highway. It looks like an interstate. That would be a lot better than ejecting or landing on the sand. What are the restrictions about landing on an interstate highway? You need a stretch of roadway that's relatively flat and straight for at least a mile. It must be void of electric transmission lines crossing the highway. I can't see any electric lines from here, but I'm still 5 miles high. You have to land in the same direction as the traffic. And that might mean landing with a tail wind. It could save the airplane, but landing at 125 miles an hour, trying to blend in with 18 wheelers at 70 miles an hour, is not easy, especially when you are a glider."

"I need to open my emergency checklist to review the engine restart procedure. There it is. OK, I will run through it before I get to 25,000."

35,000 feet...

30,000 feet...

25,000 feet…

I initiate the Air Start Procedure for the Starboard Engine:

1. PCL (Power Control Lever) - OFF

2. Purge fuel - (climb or negative "g")

3. Battery - NORM/EMERGENCY

4. Check MASTERS - ON

5. Check circuit breakers - IN

6. RPM Minimum 8%, below 25,000 feet

7. Air Start/Ignition - ON

8. PCL - IDLE

9. Monitor EGT (Exhaust Gas Temperature)

10. Air start ignition OFF

The Starboard Engine fails to start.

24,000 feet

Try to start the Port Engine.

23,000 feet

The Port Engine fails to start.

22,000 feet. I am remembering a movie, where a girl in the desert is trying to get away from the bad guys, runs to the pickup truck with her keys and tries to get its engine to start. It turns over and over but does not start. The bad guys are getting closer!

21,000 feet.

Try to start the starboard engine again.

It sputters, then FIRES UP!

CHEERS!!!

I have one engine running. I bring up the power. Cabin pressurization and heat began to return. Smiles!

I level off at 20,000 feet and I am accelerating. Yes!

Try to start the port engine again. IT FIRES UP!

SUCCESS!

"Albuquerque Center, Buckeye 303, both engines have relit. Request climb to Flight Level 370." (37,000 feet)

(I didn't want to risk going above 40,000 feet and flaming out again.)

"Buckeye 303, good news! You are cleared on course to FL 370."

I made it home safely without further incident.

Postscript:

I never messed around maneuvering the T-2 at high altitude, again. I learned my lesson. Someday I would pilot the F-4 Phantom. It would have engines that would not quit, no matter how you maneuvered. But I wasn't there yet.

Advice to my grandchildren:

1. If you're going to take a peek at something you're not supposed to look at, be prepared to pay the consequences…

2. You need to plan for the unexpected. Naval aviators rehearse for emergencies and practice them whenever they can. Most of the time, the rehearsal is mental. Then when a really difficult situation emerges, you will be prepared to handle it.

Chapter 5
The Real Top Gun

Top Gun, the 1986 Movie

Top Gun is still one of my favorite movies. Not because it's realistic. It is not. But it is entertaining and it gave me an opportunity to explain to my parents, wife, children and extended family what I did for a living. They got to see my "office," a fighter airplane cockpit, and learn something about missions we carried out. When I visited my birth town, Eau Claire, Wisconsin in the summer of 1986, I took the entire available Werner family to the theater: Mom, Dad, wife, 3 children, 6 siblings and 10 nieces and nephews. We took up two full rows of the theater during a matinee showing. It was memorable!

There are so many flaws in the movie, that I could write an entire chapter on them. Let's just discuss a few.

<u>Top Gun Trophy</u>. First, there is no top gun trophy. The writers completely missed the point. The real Navy Fighter Weapons School (Top Gun) is a train-the-trainer program. It is not a place where studs try to outdo each other to win a trophy. The real prize is being invited back to be an instructor.

<u>Troubleshooters</u>. New graduates of Top Gun are not sent out to be troubleshooters in hotspots around the world. Their job is to go back to their home squadron and teach what they learned to the other air crews, thereby improving the performance of the entire squadron.

<u>Tower fly-bys</u>. No pilot gets away with doing a flyby after the tower denies their request. Maverick would have lost his wings the first time he tried that stunt and the movie would have been over. A very short movie…

<u>Family photos</u>. No pilot flies with a photograph of his wife or child posted in the cockpit. Flying fighters and landing on an aircraft carrier are such demanding tasks, you do not want any distractions.

<u>Emotional breakdown on final approach</u>. There is no crying in flying. Anyone who is that out-of-control is washed out years earlier in officer training or flight school. In some cases, psychological testing is used to determine fitness, but usually it comes from seniors

observing how an officer candidate or student pilot behaves under pressure. This selection process saves lives and expensive equipment.

<u>Close in fight</u>. In the real world, dogfighting aircraft do not fly so close together that they can all be seen on the same screen. I understand why Hollywood did it (to tell the story in pictures) but it does not happen. The general rule of thumb is to stay a mile apart. That way you can support one another and you can't both be shot down by the same enemy airplane. You also don't get caught in the debris of your own missile when it blows up the enemy. A much more realistic fighter pilot movie was *The Great Santini*, starring Robert Duvall.

<u>Oxygen masks.</u> Nobody takes their oxygen masks off while flying jets to talk to somebody. The Hollywood director did it just so he could show off Tom Cruise's patented smile.

<u>Air combat experts</u>. Fighter pilots do not take flying or maneuvering advice from non-pilots, especially a female with no air combat experience. (The Kelly McGillis character) They do take tactical planning advice from experts, based on research.

<u>Cute saying</u>. No fighter pilot ever said "I feel the need, the need for speed!" It was invented for the movie. What we did say was "Speed is life." (With speed you have all kinds of maneuvering options,

including outrunning your enemy. Too slow, you're in trouble in a hostile environment. More about that later.)

<u>Mispronunciations.</u> Now I am really getting picky! The school is referred to as top'-gun with emphasis on the word Top, not on Gun. And "wingman" is pronounced wing'-man, with emphasis on wing not on man.

<u>What Was Realistic About The Movie?</u>

<u>Flight Operations.</u> The opening scene of flight deck operations was from a real aircraft carrier. Much of the movie's photography was taken using real aircraft flown by Navy pilots. Many scenes used models and computer generated images (CGI). None of the flying was conducted by any of the actors.

<u>Volleyball</u>. Naval aviators are athletes and are competitive in many sports, including volleyball, but they don't all have bodies like the actors in the movie.

Real fighter pilots, VF-102, 1977

<u>Groupies at the Officer's Club.</u> There are usually plenty of attractive young women looking to hook up with an aviator. As a result, the lady's room would be way too busy for Maverick to make his horny one-on-one sailor move on Kelly McGillis. Like in any busy club, there's always a long line at the ladies room.

<u>You've Lost that Loving' Feeling.</u> More than one fighter pilot, who can't sing, has tried to seduce some chick in an O' Club, with a vocal serenade. But this one has already become a classic! I liked the Maverick-Goose teamwork.

<u>Best of the best</u>. Those chosen to go to Top Gun are the best of the best, but not just the best pilots. Because it is a train-the-trainer program, they also have to be the best teachers. With a fitness report

that reads, "He's a wildcard. Completely unpredictable. Flies by the seat of his pants…" Maverick would have been removed from the Navy, not sent to Top Gun.

<u>Loss of an F-14 in a flat spin</u>. It was realistic to show that naval aviation is a dangerous business. The F-14 Tomcat can get into an unrecoverable flat spin. What the movie didn't say was that Goose failed to follow emergency procedures and jettison the canopy before pulling the ejection seat handle. If he did so, he would not have been killed. But the death drama was an important part of the movie.

The Second Top Gun Movie: Maverick 2022

Similar to the first movie, the sequel "Top Gun: Maverick" is both very entertaining and unrealistic. The premise that one pilot, Maverick, can get away with unauthorized tower flybys (in both movies), an uncleared flight that destroys a Mach 10.0 experimental aircraft, as well as stealing and intentionally over-stressing an F-18 Hornet, is totally unrealistic.

Same critique as the first movie, he would have had his Navy wings pulled the first time he buzzed a tower, without clearance. Nobody as undisciplined as Maverick makes it far in the real U.S. Navy. He would have been gone…

Now, for the realism in the new movie. The Aircraft carrier flight deck scene in the beginning is real, again. Nearly all of the flying is real.

They put the cast members through more than three months of naval aviation boot camp, where they had to prepare to handle real emergencies, including ejecting from an F-18 Super Hornet and landing by parachute on land or in water.

Most of the flying and dog fighting scenes are real, with a Navy pilot flying the airplane from the front seat of an F-18 Super Hornet, and the cast member pretending to fly from the backseat. But the actors wore the flight gear, had to breathe and communicate through a real oxygen mask and experience the same g-forces as the pilot. They felt the exhilaration of a high speed chase and dogfight. That meant, in many cases, they did not have to do much acting!

The camera work with fighter jets was the finest ever recorded. It was so real, that in the beginning of the movie when Maverick does an unauthorized takeoff in an experimental airplane, the wind from the passing aircraft actually blows the top off the guard shack. With the set having been destroyed, they had to accept the first take on that scene. It's a good thing they got it right! The actors' cockpits were also equipped with six cameras, to get close-ups from any angle. The movie makers had to work with the Navy for more than a year to make sure that none of the equipment would interfere with the function of the aircraft or the ejection seat.

The script calls for a mission to knock out an enemy country's uranium enrichment plant. That was realistic. The risks they faced in doing so were also pretty realistic. I don't agree with their approach to the mission or the tactics they used, but then I'm not a movie script writer.

On the downside, 1 found the interaction between characters similar to "reality TV." There are many strong personalities among real navy fighter pilots, but the deep respect and camaraderie were mostly missing. The actors were openly antagonistic, if not hostile towards one another. Now, that doesn't mean actual fighter pilots don't harbor some of the same feelings, but they're much more subtle and measured in their discourse. Real fighter pilots show more loyalty to one another. They value disciplined teamwork and respect experience and rank.

I recommend the movie to anyone who wants to see what it looks like to be in the cockpit of a modern fighter jet during real fast low level flying and dog fighting.

What I found missing was the love story chemistry from the first movie, between Tom Cruise and Kelly McGillis. His love life in this movie, with Jennifer Connelly, was a little boring! But that is realistic for an old fighter pilot. □

A Google search reveals that the first Top Gun movie increased naval aviation recruitment by 500%. But what those new pilots eventually learned was that the real life of a naval aviator is not always exciting. It requires a lot of family separation, hard work, discipline, and risk. The really exciting flying lasts for only minutes out of a day, while downtime lasts for hours. There are some long, boring missions, bad weather, and mechanical problems. They have to deal with occasional poor leadership, resulting in dangerous, unnecessary, and sometimes questionable missions.

And on top of all of that, Kelly McGillis never shows up at happy hour!

Movies are made for movie goers, not for fighter pilots. If I had written the script for this movie, I guarantee it would not have made $1.5 Billion in ticket sales by March 2023!

In conclusion, I gave the movie 5 stars for flying realism and 3 stars for the storyline. I had to suspend my knowledge of how things really work in order to enjoy the movie. Hopefully, you can just go along for the ride.

History of Top Gun

Source: Wikipedia - United States Navy Strike Fighter Tactics Instructor program

"In 1968, Chief of Naval Operations, Admiral Thomas Moorer, ordered research into why the US was performing so poorly in aerial combat over the skies in North Vietnam. Nearly 1000 US aircraft were lost in about 1 million sorties. In response, researchers published a report that found inadequate aircrew training was the biggest root cause. So they recommended establishing an advanced fighter weapons school at Naval Station Miramar in San Diego, California. Top Gun was Established in March, 1969."

"Top Gun's purpose was to train fighter aircrews, at the graduate level, in all aspects of fighter weapons systems, including tactics, techniques, procedures and doctrine. It served to build a nucleus of eminently knowledgeable fighter crews to construct, guide and enhance weapons training and subsequent aircrew performance. The curriculum was in a constant state of flux based on class critiques and integration of developing tactics to use new systems to combat emergent threats."

"The predominant enemy aircraft that day were the Russian-built transonic MiG-17 and the supersonic MiG-21. To simulate the performance of those aircraft, Top Gun used the A-4 Skyhawk, the T-38 Talon and eventually the F-5E and F-5F Tiger."

"Aircrews selected to attend Top Gun were chosen from frontline squadrons. The graduates were to return to their parent fleet and relay what they learned to their fellow squadron mates, in essence, become instructors themselves."

"The school turned out to be wildly successful. The kill-to-loss ratio against North Vietnamese Air Force MiGs soared (improved) from 2.42:1 to 12.5:1. The US Air Force focussed on improving technology and did not establish a training program similar to Top Gun. Their kill ratio actually got worse!"

Top Gun, 1977, San Diego, CA

Normally a Navy fighter squadron is permitted to send only one crew per year to Top Gun. F-4 Phantom and F-14 Tomcat crews consisted of a pilot and a Radar Intercept Officer (RIO). But our VF-102 commanding officer, Drex "Goober" Bradshaw decided he wanted to send two crews and got permission to do so.

The primary crew was Russ "Craze" Plappert and Bill "Nips" Foster, good friends of mine. Jerry "Disco" Werner and Larry "Vert" Neal were alternates. I didn't care. I was just delighted to be going to Top Gun. According to the Navy's own advertising, only 1% of Navy pilots attend Top Gun. The flying and competition don't get any better than this! I imagined this experience would also help in my coming competition to get into the test pilot school, a necessary step on my way to the astronaut program.

The four of us from VF-102 arrived at the Naval Air Station (NAS) Miramar on October 5, 1977, Craze, Nips, Vert and me. If we encountered any Top Gun resource limitations, Craze and Nips got first priority. As it turns out, in the five weeks we were there, Vert and I only missed one sortie because of airplane problems.

Highlighted: front row, Jerry "Disco" Werner, Greg "Tokyo" Rose, and Larry "Vert" Neal, back row, Russ "Craze" Plappert, Bill "Nips" Foster, Scott "Lumpy" Davis, and the Israelis. All to be introduced below.

While attending and participating in the Top Gun program, I was also the Officer-in-Charge (OINC) of the VF-102 Detachment of 4 Petty Officers and 36 maintenance crew responsible for the maintenance and readiness of our two and VF-33's one F-4 Phantom. All of us stayed in Navy housing on the base and our planes had their own hangar. It was extra work, but I liked the leadership part of my job. As discussed in a previous chapter, in addition to flying, Navy pilots/RIOs are also officers with collateral duties, leading departments or divisions within the squadron.

VF-102 Diamondbacks F-4J Phantoms

Our sister F-4 Phantom squadron, VF-33, also from the USS Independence, sent Greg "Tokyo" Rose and his RIO, Scott "Lumpy" Davis. We were all on the same team, but we were also competitors. For some reason, they didn't like me much. It may have had something to do with my standup comedy routine, on the aircraft carrier, when I mocked their executive officer, resulting in them being punished. See "Fo'c's'le Follies."

Our Top Gun Experience

The Navy Fighter Weapons School in 1977 was in San Diego, and consisted of both classroom and flying activities, every day. Very interesting topics. Very exciting flying.

One of the first evenings at Top Gun, Vietnam War Ace Randy "Duke" Cunningham joined all of us students for dinner. (An Ace is a pilot credited with shooting down at least five enemy airplanes.) He gave us a presentation, told his stories of battles in the skies over Vietnam and stayed for drinks and Q&A. A year later, I would do a parody of his stories to roast him at the annual fighter pilot's ball, the Fighter Fling. Duke was a good sport about it. Randy would go on to be elected to the US Congress from California. Eventually, he got himself in trouble and ended up in prison. He was found guilty of accepting bribes from military contractors.

In my opinion, the reason Top Gun was so successful in improving the win percentage was because they taught pilots how to fight as a team, not just how to win a one-on-one battle. And to fight as a team, you had to learn how to call out the location of the enemy using three-dimensional positions, from the perspective of your teammate's aircraft, not your own.

"Bogey, your left 11 o'clock high!"

"Bandit level with you, right 3 o'clock."

"He's closing in on you, right 5 o'clock low. Break starboard now!"

To be a trainer of other fighter pilots in "dog fighting," you also had to learn how to remember an entire flight, turn-by-turn in three dimensions and then recreate it on a white board. You needed to be able to describe how some maneuvers were done well and how others could be improved. We drew a vertical line down the middle of the whiteboard and listed "Good" on the left side and "Other" on the right side. We wrote down everything about the flight that was positive on the left and things that needed improvement on the right side of the board.

The goal was to help the student learn and improve, not to embarrass or humiliate anyone for their mistakes. These observations became opportunities upon which to build. At first, I didn't think I was going to be able to remember 45 minutes of encounters, turn by turn, with only mental notes. But surprisingly I learned how and got pretty good at it.

Some Flying Highlights

<u>First Top Gun flight</u>.

In my very first flight, dog fighting one-on-one with the F-5E Tiger flown by a Top Gun instructor, I got my ass kicked. In the debriefing following the flight, he told us that if we want to win a dogfight flying an F-4, we cannot get into a flat turning fight with an F-5 or a MiG. They can both easily outturn you. The only way to beat either aircraft would be to use the F-4 Phantom's superior climb performance. In order to leverage that advantage, the pilot needs to know how to maximize his climb and reverse course at the top of the climb. The instructor only knew one pilot, many years ago, who could do a vertical reversal in an F-4. He had no clue how he did it.

Jerry Werner

Northrop F-5E Tiger

Mastering the Vertical Reversal

Learning how to do a vertical reversal became my own homework obsession. I took advantage of my position as the officer-in-charge of our little unit and commandeered an airplane at the end of the workday. Instead of going to happy hour, Vert and I flew out over the ocean, in the designated military operating area, where we tried to figure out how to use the superior climb of the F-4 and do a vertical reversal.

We were working on a mystery without any clues. I tried repeatedly to fly straight up in the vertical, but was unsuccessful. I finally decided to use the globe-shaped attitude indicator that we focused on to keep the wings level when we fly in the clouds. By aligning the cross-hairs exactly on the dot at the top of the "sky," we were theoretically in the pure vertical.

Then we had to figure out how and when to initiate the reversal. I waited till we slowed to zero airspeed, and that was way too late. Control was already lost. The airplane fell off unpredictably, like an autumn maple leaf, or dropped straight down backwards, forcing air up into the exhaust of the engines. That did not cause any damage to the engines, but it did delay getting pointed downhill and flying again. Not good!

I experimented initiating the reversal at various speeds, 50, 100, 150, 200, but none of them worked. I ended up hovering in the sky at zero air speed at least a dozen times. I could not get the nose to point down at the earth when I wanted it to. We flew back home discouraged.

Larry said, "Disco, I've never spent so much time at zero airspeed. We could've gotten a parking ticket!"

We skipped happy hour the next day and tried again. Another half dozen failures. Then, finally we figured out the secret. One needs to accelerate to a high speed like 600 knots minimum in full afterburner, pull the airplane straight up in the sky, and when it decelerates to 250 knots, bring throttles back to idle, neutralize the stick, then apply full rudder pedal deflection. Result: The nose of the F-4 swings neatly straight down, still under control, and we were off to the races downhill!

"Hey, Vert, we figured it out! Shit Hot!"

On the third day, we skipped happy hour again just to go out and practice the reversal over and over again. We perfected it and never lost a one-on-one fight after that, even against the Top Gun instructors in their F-5s. All but one of the instructors said they had never seen the move before. That gave me the impression that Larry and I were likely the only ones in the Navy who knew how to do it.

How to Win a Dogfight with the F-4

How does this maneuver allow the F-4 to beat every other aircraft - of that time - in a dog fight? The F-4 Phantom (the climb champion) climbs so high, so fast that other airplanes chasing it cannot keep up, run out of poop, and fall back to earth. When my RIO sees them fall off, he calls, "Disco, reverse now!" I reverse, accelerate downhill and quickly close in for the kill. It works even better when you can get the enemy to follow you up into the sun, where he gets blinded and loses sight of you, atactic as old as World War I.

F-4 Phantom, with afterburners, headed vertical

This maneuver was classified in 1977, but all American F-4s have since been decommissioned, so we are safe in revealing this. I shared the vertical reversal technique with my VF-102 squadron mates, as was the expectation upon returning from Top Gun. Some, but not all, gave it a try.

When we participated in the annual readiness evaluation by VF-43, their pilots also said that they had never seen the move before. I beat them every time. They were so impressed that they asked me to officially share with the entire U.S. Navy F-4 Phantom community. I just reread my submission, for the purpose of writing this book. I was surprised to find that I left out a key number, the air speed at which to begin on the reversal. Did I just forget to include it or was I really that competitive that I intentionally withheld that secret? I don't remember…

Too low

Every day was fun and exciting, flying at Top Gun. One of the most exciting was low-level high speed across the Mojave Desert. It was one of those One vs. Many fights (every man for himself) when we were looking for a target of opportunity. We decided if we stayed low enough and fast enough, all of our targets of opportunity would be in front of and above us. But I got a little too low at 600 knots. I looked out and saw that we were below the cactus tops.

At the same time, Vert came up on the ICS and said,

"Hey Disco, we're kicking up a dust storm back here! Pull up a bit!"

I wasn't that low!

I did pop up for safety sake. Minutes later, our plan proved successful. A bogey appeared above and in front of us on Vert's radar. I found him visually.

"Tally ho!"

Vert locked him up. I centered him in the gun site and pulled the simulated trigger,

"Fox 2!"

and shot down the unsuspecting bad guy with a simulated heat-seeking AIM-9 Sidewinder missile. The same type of missile used to shoot down the Chinese spy balloon in 2023.

Friendly Fire

Our scariest experience at Top Gun happened in the last week of the program, on the last flight of the day, during a 2 vs. 1 missile exercise. The mission was to work as a section (a two-aircraft, 4-man team, flying F-4 Phantoms) and fire a live radar-guided AIM-7 Sparrow missile at a drone. We called it a drone, but it was actually an RPV (Remotely Piloted Vehicle). 99% of the time, we used simulation when firing missiles at an "enemy" airplane. But this was the real thing. This was a missile that could kill you.

I have given our buddies a fake call sign, "Ghostwriter," to conceal their true identity. They had the lead and we were their wingman. To be a wingman means to fly in a separate airplane, coordinating with them as teammates. Our goal was to approach the drone, as if it were an enemy aircraft, and use the team tactics we learned at Top Gun to successfully shoot it down.

We took off together from NAS Miramar. We proceeded to the operating area and waited for the drone to show up. The drone pilot on the ground was having some problems communicating with the RPV and with us. They were late. We were in a holding pattern until they arrived.

Finally after about a half hour wait, we were notified that the drone had arrived and that the operating area was officially "hot." We were cleared to fire. I flew on Ghostwriter's wing, about 1 mile abreast. The visibility was not perfect and the RPV was so small, compared with aircraft that we usually fight, that neither RIO could find it on their radar. Then suddenly we saw it zip past between us and we F-4s started a turning, rolling dog fight with the drone. Ghostwriter was in a better location to turn on the drone and get into position to shoot. So I maneuvered into a supportive spot, about 5000 feet above them.

In the heat of the battle, Ghostwriter lost sight of us, armed their missile and locked their aircraft's radar onto what they thought was the drone. Picture the sky with Ghostwriter at the bottom, the drone in the middle and Disco/Vert at the top of the circle. We didn't know it at the time, but Ghostwriter's radar was not locked on the drone. It was actually locked onto the much bigger target in the same line-of-sight - US!

If we had active Electronic Counter Measures (ECM) gear, we would have heard the shrill sound of the radar lock on us and could have alerted them to their mistake. If we had chaff (as a decoy), we would have been able to deploy it to fool the missile. We had neither. We weren't expecting someone to be shooting a live missile at us that day!

Ghostwriter pressed the trigger, and called out "Fox 1!"

The "Fox 1" radio call was the signal to everyone that the Sparrow missile was being fired and the RPV pilot should make a hard turn to try to defeat the missile and save the drone for another day of target practice.

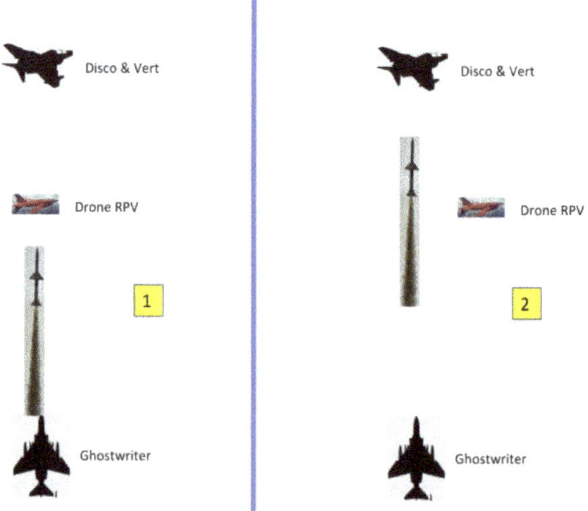

From high above, I rolled over to look out to see what was happening below us.

I saw the Sparrow missile launch off its rails spewing fire and smoke. It shot up in the direction of the drone that was turning hard right. Then the missile went right past the drone and headed up towards us. I saw it coming. I was preparing to eject. With enough speed in an F-4, you can out-maneuver a missile, but we were way too slow. (Remember: "Speed is life?") We were sitting ducks!

As it came closer, my left hand approached the ejection handle, but there were no good options. If I waited too long to eject, we would be blown up. If I ejected immediately at that angle, we might eject ourselves right into the missile's path.

Then, finally the nose of the missile, about 100 yards from us, went ballistic, dropping away in a parabola down towards the water below.

WHEW! (Exhale…)

(This whole episode took less than 10 seconds.)

Thank God! (It wasn't our day to die!)

"Sonofabitch! That was close!" I said to Vert.

We were fortunate that the F-4J radar system was one of the worst in the world. (AWG-10 by Westinghouse) Ghostwriter's

AWG-10 radar had apparently lost its lock on our aircraft in the nick of time!

I did not say anything over the radio. Nobody knew what happened but the four of us. The controller of the drone could not "see" what happened on the radar. He did not hear anything, except our acknowledgment that the missile missed the drone. There was no incriminating recording.

The mission that day called for both crews to get a chance to shoot a live missile. But we had run out of time and low on fuel. Due to all the delays in getting started, we had to head back home.

This incident became our secret. Best to keep it that way. It could've ruined Ghostwriter's career. I decided to handle it with a conversation at happy hour, where we always debriefed the last flight of the day. But, they didn't show up to happy hour that evening or the rest of our time at Top Gun. They knew what they had done wrong and would not repeat it. (Ghostwriter pilot and I eventually become friends.)

Social Life in San Diego

I am writing this book for my grandchildren and I'm not going to pretend that I was a saint. I was a fighter pilot in the US Navy. We occasionally drank too much, we cursed, we flirted, and we told off-color stories. Some vices my buddies at Top Gun avoided: We did not cheat on our wives, we did not smoke cigarettes or did illegal drugs and we religiously followed the Navy drinking guidelines of, "12 hours from bottle to throttle."

Against that backdrop, for the six weeks we were in San Diego, we Diamondbacks from VF-102 went out together just about every night. Larry "Vert" Neal, Russ "Craze" Plappert, Bill "Nips" Foster, and me. We went to Happy Hour at the Miramar Officers Club or the Marine Corps Officers Club, dinners and margaritas at the Mexican restaurant Su Casa, dinner and rum n' cokes at the 94th Aero Squadron. I had a great time socializing with those guys.

The locals, in the San Diego area, were very friendly and welcoming. It was my first really positive experience with the public since the end of the Vietnam War, January 27, 1973. We veterans were not treated well after the war ended. I believe that's one of the reasons why so many people now say to us, "Thank you for your service."

As the officer-in-charge, I organized a softball game and picnic one Saturday for the 40 sailors and four officers. I don't remember whose team won, but I do remember hitting a triple and racing around the diamond to third base. By the time I got there, my lungs were burning from breathing smog. I'd never experienced that before or since, even living in New York City. In spite of the air quality, we all had a good time.

Another day, the guys invited me to join them at Black's Beach, where clothing was optional. I declined. After all, I was a modest Catholic boy.

Our Israeli Classmates

We had two Top Gun classmates from Israel. I have withheld their names. They were not very friendly and kept to themselves. I tried to engage them in conversation more than once. I asked them to join us socially, but they declined. It could've been culture. It could've been religion. It could've been language, but as it turns out, it was something else.

It was clear, the Israelis thought Americans were pampered. They didn't think Americans appreciated the risks Israel faced.

"Americans live in a big, rich, powerful country surrounded by friends and lots of water. Israelis live in a small country surrounded by lots of enemies who want to wipe us off the map."

They criticized us for not taking Memorial Day seriously,

"Instead of honoring the dead, Americans go shopping!"

The most surprising thing the Israelis told me was that I should watch my back, because someday I might find them at 6 o'clock. It didn't make sense until, in 2020, Larry Neal told me that those two Israeli men participated in the 1981 raid on the Iraqi nuclear plant at Osiraq near Baghdad. He said that one of them led it. That officer later became a senior member of the Israeli Air Force. And that raid, along with an attack on Iran's nuclear facility, was condemned by both the United States and the United Nations. (The USA was on friendly terms with both Iraq and Iran at that time.)

So the Israelis were telling me that, under normal conditions, we were allies. But when it came to protecting their own country and destroying their neighbor's nuclear weapons development, they would operate on their own, and shoot me down, if I got in their way. (But they would have to counter my vertical reversal, first!)

Action Plan, Back Home

VF-102 Diamondbacks Home Base at NAS Oceana, VA 1977

Our Skipper, Commander Drex Bradshaw, welcomed us home. He said that he had a conversation with the Top Gun commanding officer, JC Smith. Their CO had glowing compliments for the four of us but Smith said his instructors had voted Werner the best pilot of the entire class. CDR Bradshaw thanked us for representing him and the Diamondbacks so well.

He asked us what we had learned. He showed interest in everything we told him, but there were three topics that became his action items.

- First was the vertical reversal. He wanted Larry and me to teach it to the squadron pilots.

- Second was camouflage for the airplanes. Top Gun recommended a new paint scheme that would make it harder for the enemy to identify us.

- Third, to discontinue the failing Vietnam War tactics, such as flying a gaggle of airplanes into enemy territory at a medium altitude, called an "Alpha Strike.". Our planes were all at risk of being shot down by surface to air missiles and anti-aircraft fire. We had to coordinate as a team, with the entire air wing, and conduct low level stream raids, avoiding enemy detection, and capitalize on surprise. This was demonstrated pretty well in the 2022 movie Top Gun: Maverick.

CDR Bradshaw then said he wanted us to meet with the Carrier Air Group Commander (CAG) and tell him what we had learned. CAG is responsible for all 100 airplanes that are deployed to an aircraft carrier. It's his job to see that they all work together as one big team. He would make his recommendations to CAG before we met with him, but it would be good for him to hear directly from us.

A couple of days later, I was handed a phone message. I returned the call. It was an instructor at Top Gun.

"Lieutenant Werner, my CO asked me to give you a call and let you know the good news. All the instructors took a vote on who they would like to return to Top Gun as an instructor and you were our unanimous choice. Congratulations!"

I told him, "I am honored! Please thank the Skipper and your fellow instructors. I thought you and they did an excellent job. I would love to join you all as a Top Gun instructor, if I don't get into test pilot school. But my first choice is test pilot school."

Within a week, the Carrier Air Group Commander invited us to meet with him, as arranged. It was the first time I was asked by a senior person for my opinion, with the intention to put it into action. And I was not quite 30 years old yet. Actually, I was passing on the opinion of Top Gun and naval air researchers, but it felt good to be asked. This was December 1977 and our CAG changed his War Plan to focus on low level stream raids, rather than coming in with a big group of airplanes at 15,000 feet.

Unfortunately, he was not the CAG when President Reagan sent American forces from the USS Kennedy and USS Independence to attack Syrians in Lebanon in 1983 with 24 US Navy war planes. Some ill-informed leaders, apparently not trained at Top Gun, sent those airplanes into the fight, using the outdated Vietnam war tactics instead of stream raids. Washington also did not give the ships involved enough time to configure all the aircraft appropriately. They paid a big price for it. Two airplanes were shot down, others were damaged, and one man became a prisoner of war, and another was dead.

The good news that came out of that fiasco? It was the understanding that everybody needed better training, not just fighter pilots at Top Gun. So the Navy formed The Naval Strike and Air Warfare Center (Strike-U) at NAS Fallon, Nevada. The mission of Strike-U is to make sure that everybody is up-to-date with the latest strategy, tactics and training. Not just fighter pilots.

Postscript

Getting invited back to Top Gun as an instructor would certainly bolster my resume/fitness report and increase my chances of getting the appointment to test pilot school.

How did my squadron mates do with trying the vertical reversal? I think it's fair to say that everybody became more conscious that the dogfight needs to be vertical, not horizontal. But I don't know anyone else who mastered the vertical reversal. I gave them the formula and coaching, but they still had difficulty with it. I reminded them that I spent 3 full flights, 4.5 hours of practice to perfect it. I don't think they wanted to invest that much time. I also had another advantage. I had been the main spin recovery instructor at VT-9 and I was very comfortable with an airplane at zero air speed and highly confident that I could recover from any kind of spin.

Note to Grandchildren:

1. Don't get disappointed if you are chosen as an *alternate*. With the right determination and willingness to work (i.e., perfect a vertical reversal), you can still come out on top!

2. When someone makes a serious mistake, (shoot at you with a live missile), but nobody gets hurt, sometimes it's better just to let it sink in. They know their error. Let them learn and move on from it.

Chapter 6

Time to Buzz the Tower?

This story is about one of the most fun flights in my entire life, but it does have a scary ending.

I was flying F-4J Phantom, Tail Number 155767 on Sunday, May 14, 1978, with Larry "Vert" Neal in my backseat. We were stationed with the VF-102 Diamondbacks out of Naval Air Station Oceana, Virginia Beach, VA. Larry and I flew many flights together. He was my favorite Radar Intercept Officer (RIO) and we had just completed a very successful mission at Top Gun in December. We were both at the top of our game and did not consider what we were about to do to be the least bit foolhardy.

One of the most exciting things about flying a really fast airplane is doing it close to the ground. We flew high speed, low level, terrain-hugging flights on occasion, but U.S. Navy pilots never got the chance to do a low level high speed tower fly-by at an air base unless we were part of an air show. Generally, airports and their surroundings are just too crowded to do it safely. I had not had the opportunity to do one before.

I didn't know it yet, but here was my opportunity. We were at the Air National Guard base, Volk Field, Camp Douglas, in Central Wisconsin. The field could be very busy in the summer, but it was absolutely deserted that day. No other aircraft were on the ground or in the air. Actually, we were the only aircraft operating the whole weekend. They even put our Phantom in a warm hangar, so we didn't have to do a cold outdoor pre-flight. I appreciated that. Even though it was May, the overnight temperature was below freezing.

Larry and I came to visit my family in the Eau Claire area on Friday. I wanted to land at the airport in Eau Claire, but the runway was too short and they were not equipped to handle military airplanes. So we planned the flight into Volk Field. My dad picked us up from Volk on Friday and drove us back to the Guard base on Sunday morning, about a 90 minute trip. Mom and my sisters joined us. They were going to watch us take off.

There was no ground radio communication with Air Traffic Control (ATC) at Volk Field, so we filed our flight plan back to NAS Oceana over a land line. We would activate the flight plan on the radio with Chicago Center after we were airborne.

The National Guard ground personnel were wonderful. They were Wisconsin-friendly. They let us bring our family to the hangar and show them the airplane. They helped us pre-flight the aircraft inside the warm hangar and waited until we had climbed into our cockpits to tow us outside to start.

They attached the big hose from the huffer that blew hot air through the engines to start them up. I've always found it exciting to start up the engines on any airplane. Why? Because we are going flying! But nothing matched the adrenaline rush of starting up the F-4 Phantom, the feeling of having such monstrously powerful motors, 36,000 pounds of thrust, swirling beneath you. I felt good about finally getting the chance to visit my home state and show off this amazing machine.

Starting the engines on an F-4 Phantom

After completing our pre-taxi checks, Larry contacted ground control and requested clearance to taxi to the active runway. They cleared us to taxi to the westbound runway, RWY 27.

Our taxi and takeoff path at Volk Field

While taxiing, I said to Larry, "Hey Vert, considering this place is deserted today, I wonder if they would let us do a flyby."

Larry said, "There's only one way to find out. I will give them a call."

"Ground, Diamondback 103, request a low flyby after takeoff."

There was a long pause and then the youngsters in the tower responded enthusiastically:

"Diamondback 103, Ground, low fly-by approved!"

I heard somebody yell "Yippee!" in the background. Apparently, off-season weekends were a little boring.

Tower personnel

At this point, I need to remind you that a pilot cannot do a low fly-by without permission from the tower and that goes for Tom Cruise (Maverick in Top Gun) and everybody else. If Maverick had pulled that stunt in the real Navy, he would have lost his wings the first time and, as I have said before, it would have been a very short first movie with no sequel.

After being cleared for takeoff, I taxied onto the runway. We did our final checks. I went to military power, then full afterburner.

Pow - Pow!

The two afterburners ignited and we accelerated down the runway and lifted off around 180 mph.

After takeoff I came out of afterburner and we popped up to 1000 feet, heading straight west over I-94 and the countryside. I told the tower that I would fly out to 10 miles before turning around. That would give us plenty of room to accelerate for our flyby.

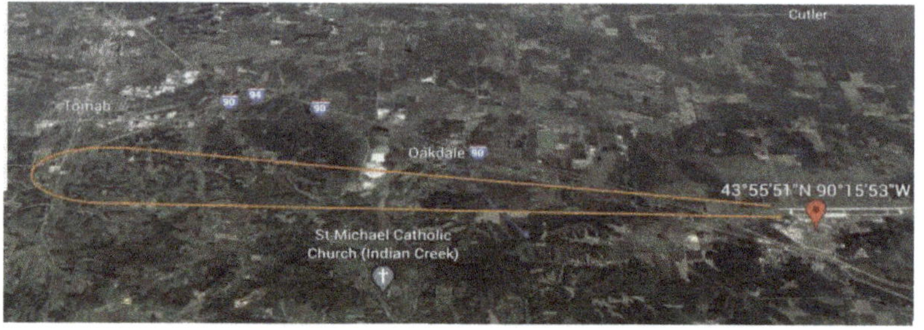

Path flown west of Volk Field

On our way out to 10 miles, I saw a chicken coop below us. I was wondering if we had awakened the chickens or if the rooster had done so at dawn. Would our noise affect their egg production today?

We crossed near a white farmhouse with a red barn and silo. I wanted to make sure to alter my path on the way back, so as not to disturb them again. The family could be getting ready to go to church. I remembered my days working on farms and how different my life was then.

At 10 miles out, I turned around and headed back towards the airbase in full afterburner. I did a gradual descent, accelerating rapidly. By the time we reached the field boundary, we were below 100 feet and haulin' ass at 600 knots! (690 mph)

F-4 Phantom high speed, low level

I aimed straight at the tower and pulled up into the vertical in front of them, just like the Blue Angels at an airshow.

F-4 Phantom in vertical climb

The youngsters in the tower saw us screaming right at them, zip up in a climb with flames under us like a rocket. We rattled their tower windows with a thunderous roar! They keyed their mic and excitedly screamed,

"HOLY SHIT!"

We heard clapping in the background! We must have made their day!

We vaulted into a vertical climb, shooting up through 20,000 feet in about 20 seconds!

My family saw the show from their car on the way home on I-94. They told us later that it was spectacular. They waved. Of course, we couldn't see them…

OK, it was a pretty good show on the ground, but

"Houston, we have a problem."

I did not expect thick cloud cover. We entered a cloud deck and never came out on top. Once I realized that we were climbing through 20,000 feet, still in the clouds, without a clearance from air traffic control, I knew we had to get back down below 18,000 feet, quickly. So, from the vertical, I slid the throttle's back to idle and pulled the nose down to the horizon where we were upside down, and then I rolled upright so we could descend down through the clouds in a dignified manner.

Wow! That maneuver really screwed up my inner ear fluid! It induced the most wicked vertigo ever! I felt like I was tumbling in space… We were still in the soup, and I had to really focus on the instruments to make sure that we were upright, stable and flying safely. Larry's senses were just as messed up.

Once we were in the clear below 18,000 feet, Larry came up on the intercom, and said:

"Hey Disco, let's never do that again."

I never did...

Postscript:

What we did was a bit crazy and I don't recommend that you try this at home. While I was focused on flying fast and zooming up into the sky, I forgot that the F-4 Phantom held 16 world records, including time to climb from sea level to 41,000 feet in one minute! I was accustomed to starting my zoom climbs above 10,000 feet where the air is much thinner. (Jet engines love cold, dense air.) Starting our climb near sea level and 700 mph, we raced through 20,000 feet so fast it made my head spin. Literally!!

Another thing I did not pay attention to was the changing weather. The high clouds came in while we were pre-flighting and I did not notice them.

Could we have hit another airplane? The chances of a collision were near zero (there was no air traffic in the area and no airways above the airport), but it was still breaking the rules.

Pilots in the USA are not permitted to fly above 18,000 feet unless they have a clearance to do so from air traffic control. Once we were back below 18,000 feet, Larry called Chicago Center, activated our flight plan and we headed home to Virginia Beach. Chicago Center never said anything about us punching a hole in their air space. It happened so fast I'm sure they did not notice.

Was there a chance of losing control of the airplane because of an unusual attitude in the clouds, upside down with rapidly deteriorating air speed? No, because I was an excellent instrument pilot, a former jet flight instructor and had recent experience doing vertical reversals at Top Gun. But it could definitely have been a dangerous maneuver for a less experienced pilot.

My son Matt asked if I could have gotten in trouble with my Commanding Officer like Maverick did in Top Gun. He was threatened with reassignment to flying cargo planes full of rubber dogshit out of Hong Kong, a non-existent billet made up for the movie. Certainly, I could have been reprimanded, but I had been cleared by the tower for the flyby, unlike Maverick who continued to buzz the tower after permission was denied.

It was our secret. Larry and I never told anyone the story, until after we were out of the Navy.

Chapter 7
We Lost What?!

Play Time

It was a warm sunny day in the Caribbean 100 miles east of Puerto Rico, January 27, 1978. It was one of those days when we were grateful to have such nice weather while it was cold and snowy back in the States.

We were flying in an F-4J Phantom (No. 107) with the VF-102 Diamondbacks off the USS Eisenhower (CVN-69). The "Ike" was brand new… the first billion dollar boat. Ours was the first Air Wing to conduct regular flight operations on the carrier.

USS Eisenhower (CVN-69)

My favorite RIO was in my backseat, Larry "Vert" Neal. We had just finished an awesome time at Top Gun in Miramar, CA. I could not have asked for a better teammate. We didn't know it, yet, but our teamwork was about to be put to its biggest test.

We had a chance for the first time to do some aerial combat (dog fighting) with our Airwing's A-7 Corsair squadron. The A-7 is a subsonic light attack bomber that replaced the A-4 Skyhawk. Built by the Vought corporation, it looked a lot like its bigger brother, the F-8 Crusader. Compared with our F-4 Phantom, it wasn't very fast, but it could turn sharply and we knew we would get beat if we got into a flat turning fight with the A-7.

F-4J Phantom (top) and A-7 Corsair (bottom)

Larry and I were fresh off the world's best training at Top Gun and were at the pinnacle of our game. We could beat anybody. So our planned 1-on-1 skirmish with the A-7 was mostly for entertainment. We showed them a few of our best moves, like slashing attacks and vertical reversals, where we could easily beat them. Then, to be fair, we allowed ourselves to get into a close-in fight so they could gain an advantage with their much better turn radius. We were maintaining good PR with our shipmates! (We wouldn't give the same consideration to our sister F-4 squadron VF-33. They were our mortal enemies…)

Rude Awakening

It was fun mixing it up with the A-7. A little too much fun. We lost track of time and were notified that we were late for rendezvous with the aircraft carrier. We raced back…too fast, the A-7 could not keep up with us. I went into the break, turning into the flight pattern for our approach and landing.

I was fast all the way and I landed long and our hook missed the wires. (That's called a "bolter.") I shoved the throttles to full power, as always on touchdown, and we jumped back in the air. Then I heard words I will never forget:

Air Boss: *"107, you've lost your starboard main mount."*

107: "Say again!"

Air Boss: "107, you lost your starboard main mount."

107: "Roger."

(He was telling us that the right side tire, wheel and shock absorber assembly had fallen off into the sea after we lifted back up in the air from the bolter. The F-4 has tricycle landing gear, a big main wheel under each wing and a pair of smaller nose gear tires in front. This was a significant impairment. We would not be able to circle and land aboard the aircraft carrier, as planned.)

I climbed in a left turn above pattern altitude to stay out of the way of other aircraft and circled overhead to await instructions.

My first thoughts, this can't be happening to us. This just a bad dream? Pinch me!

Then it settled in. Oh no, it is real. We are in dire straits. There is no easy way out of this...

107: "Please advise."

What Were the Options?

The air boss asked us how much fuel we had left and Larry told him. Our commanding officer, Drex "Goober" Bradshaw, came up on the radio very quickly and ran through the options with us.

We discussed three options. One: Land aboard the aircraft carrier, with arresting cables removed and get caught by a big net called the barricade. But our squadron mates, Brian Hurst and Denny O'Malley, died the year before when their F-4 sliced right through the nylon webbing. That option was discarded.

Option 2: Fly our aircraft at a safe altitude near the aircraft carrier and eject. But there are big risks with the rocket seat ejection system. It can break your neck, break your back, slice off your arms or fail in other ways that can kill you. Regardless, the airplane would be lost to the bottom of the sea. That option was also discarded.

Option 3: Fly to the nearest land base, the Naval Air Station at Roosevelt Roads, Puerto Rico. We had just enough gas to get there. This became the plan.

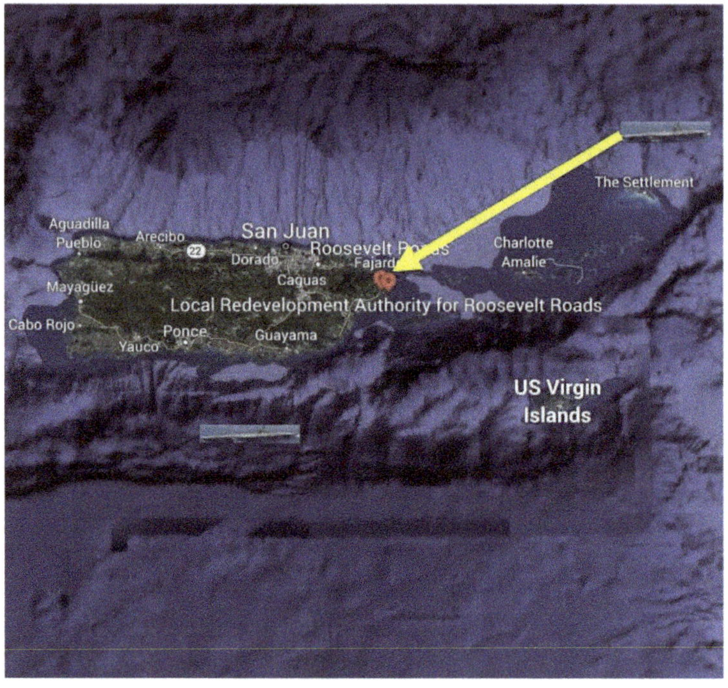

Path from USS Eisenhower to NAS Roosevelt Roads

Our CO reminded us that we would have to jettison any ordnance before we began our trip. Anything could happen when you land an airplane on a concrete runway with a stump of steel instead of a rubber tire. The airplane could swerve, tumble, or cartwheel down the runway. We couldn't take the chance of having something explode under us. We were carrying no bombs, just one heat-seeking Sidewinder (AIM-9) missile. We made sure it was unarmed. We checked to see that the ocean surface below us was clear and there were no boats. When we were sure it was OK, I pressed the button and it fell below and splashed safely into the sea.

Fly to Puerto Rico

Air Boss: "Diamondback 107, your BINGO is NAS Roosevelt Roads, 240 Degrees at 102 nautical miles. We will send a tanker to rendezvous with you." (BINGO is an order to land at a specific airfield when an aircraft is in an emergency/critical fuel situation.)

From his Emergency Checklist, Larry ran the bingo flight profile numbers. We would have to leave our landing gear down ("dirty") the entire trip, because of the risk of them not coming back down if retracted. The "dirty bingo" profile directed us to climb all the way up to 30,000 feet (most efficient use of fuel), where we could more or less coast into Puerto Rico for the final 40 miles. But it was going to be tight. We had enough fuel for one approach to the runway. If a tanker didn't show up to give us more fuel, we would have to make a perfect approach, first try.

We began our climb to 30,000 feet and were handed off to the air traffic controller responsible for the air space we would be flying through between the aircraft carrier and the land base. We were squawking 7700. (The transponder code that indicates to air traffic control that we have an emergency) We had four things we were going to request from air traffic control. We wanted them to notify NAS Roosevelt Roads to have emergency vehicles standing by, remove the wire crossing the approach end of the runway (arresting cable), foam the runway for fire suppression, and direct the refueling tanker to orbit overhead and wait for us. But we were short on time. We would be there in about a half hour.

No Help from Air Traffic Control

Then one of the most peculiar things happened. Air traffic control refused to help us when we declared an emergency! It's their job to move heaven and earth to clear a path for an aircraft in extremis to get to their destination safely. That did not happen. In spite of squawking 7700 and being notified in the handoff from USS Eisenhower that we had an emergency, we could not get the controller AFWTF's attention on the radio.

107: "Approach, Diamondback 107, requesting emergency assistance."

AFWTF: "Aircraft calling approach, standby!" AFWTF then continued a lengthy conversation with a Navy P-3 about Customs forms and box lunches... Blah, blah, blah...

Larry interrupted them again.

107: "Approach, Diamondback 107, I repeat, we have an emergency and need assistance!"

AFWTF: "Aircraft calling Approach, I said standby! Standby means NOT to talk!"

We were way too short on time to put up with such nonsense.

107: "Roger, switching to Roosevelt Roads tower." (If the controller wanted to help us, he knew where to find us: Tower frequency or Mayday frequency. He never called. A week later, he received a reprimand for his performance that day.)

Without any help or coordination from approach control, we were going to have to make it on our own. But the sky was clear to the moon, so we could fly the whole trip Visual Flight Rules, see and avoid other traffic, without air traffic control.

Larry called the tower at NAS Roosevelt Roads. We were still too far away. But because we were at such a high altitude, he kept trying and was able to talk to them from much farther away than usual, about 50 miles. He requested they have emergency vehicles standing by, remove the arresting cable from the approach end of the runway, foam the runway and tell any tanker that showed up to circle overhead. Tower told us to expect to land on Runway 07.

We used this time to thoroughly discuss how we were going to do the landing. We recalculated the fuel and it looked like we had a little more than expected, enough to do a practice approach first and then a final landing. I wanted to land with as little fuel as possible - minimize the size of a fireball, if something went wrong.

In addition to the steps in the written procedure, given light winds, I also decided to deploy the drogue chute on final approach so that it would help stabilize the airplane in a straight line and slow us down quickly after we landed. (The F-4 drogue chute is a parachute that is normally released out the back of the aircraft to slow the airplane after landing, similar to what was used on the Space Shuttle.)

We talked through our plan. I would land on the left side of the runway, away from the missing wheel. I would do a flared soft landing on the good wheel, left side and hold the right wing up, as long as I could. I would engage nose gear steering immediately after landing and use judicious braking on the left side to match the deceleration of the steel grinding on the runway on the right side, without blowing the good tire, and without swerving off the runway. Good luck! (And God help us!)

The airport came into view around 20 miles. It was a beautiful site. But as we got closer and closer, it did not look like the runway was foamed. Larry called them to confirm. The runway was NOT foamed. They don't do that anymore... Really?? How about a tanker? Nope... Arresting cable removed from runway? Nope. Emergency vehicles? Not yet.... WOW! We *were* on our own!

The tower cleared us to land on runway 07, winds were calm. I told him I would be doing a practice low approach first and then a final approach.

The practice approach gave me an opportunity to see the whole environment, make sure my airspeed was right, pick the point of landing on the runway (beyond the arresting cable) and talk through the procedures one more time with Larry. With the practice approach complete, I circled for the final approach.

Execute the Plan!

Here we go! This is it! Put the drogue chute out. Check Flaps still down. Stabilize airspeed at 145 knots (167 mph). Aim for a spot on the runway beyond the arresting cable. Pull the stick back to a smooth flared soft landing on the left side of the runway. Touchdown on the left wheel! Hold the right wing up as long as possible! Engage nose gear steering. Apply moderate to heavy breaking on the left side. Steer the aircraft in a straight line!

TOUCHDOWN! HOLD UP THE RIGHT SIDE! HOLD IT UP, HOLD IT UP!

Larry looks in his rear view mirror and sees a shower of sparks flying out from underneath the right wing caused by steel grinding on concrete at 150 miles an hour! The aircraft urgently tugs right towards that heavy friction, but fortunately, left wheel braking and nose wheel steering hold the airplane aligned with the middle of the runway and we grind swiftly to a halt.

Yay! No runway excursion! No cart wheel! No fireball! We are still alive!

We unstrap and jump out of the airplane as emergency vehicles descend upon us. We get a safe distance away from the plane and give each other the world's biggest bear hug!

We looked at the stub main mount and the runway. The runway glistened with the layer of metal that had ground off the steel landing gear door. The landing gear door looked like it had been shortened by about a foot and a half!

Celebration

We got word back from the USS Eisenhower that people were jubilant. Very happy we made it alive and saved the airplane. Some were praying for us. I appreciate that. It probably helped.

We lost the wheel because of internal salt water corrosion. It was a problem already identified with the older F-4 Phantoms. 107 was on a schedule to be inspected. Our Air Wing Commander made sure all of his F-4s were inspected before anyone else flew another sortie.

The line crew transported us to the Bachelor Officer Quarters (BOQ). We called our wives, at home in Virginia Beach. Chris and Sue were good friends. We let them know that we were fine. Of course they did not know about the incident and we shared a version that minimized the drama. No reason to make them worry anymore than they already did.

After checking in, we went to Friday night happy hour at the Officers Club, to celebrate Stayin' Alive! (Courtesy- of the Bee Gees) I was looking forward to my favorite drink, Puerto Rican white rum with Coca Cola. But pilots don't carry wallets with them when flying off an aircraft carrier, so we had no money.

Navy Nurses

Fortunately, two lovely young US Navy nurses showed up, listened to our story, and offered to pay for our drinks. I told them we would repay them when we got our things from the carrier the next day. No problem.

The nurses, 23 yr. old Navy LTjgs, from Portsmouth Naval Hospital, Virginia, were on a weekend getaway, having caught a free flight on a Navy transport. They did not live far from us back home.

They were very pleasant, engaging company and obviously smart, because they laughed at all of my jokes! We discovered that all four of us liked to play tennis. So we agreed to meet the next day to play a few sets. That would also give us a chance to repay them for drinks and dinner.

Early the next morning, Saturday, our squadron's maintenance crew arrived from the aircraft carrier. ASW First Class Teddy Dumont was in charge. They had spare parts to fix our plane and one brown bag each for Larry and me, packed by our roommates back on the ship.

I'm sure our buddies were happy that we were still alive and well, but that didn't mean that they were going to miss a chance to pull a prank on their fellow junior officers. They sent Larry only one shirt, his King Kong T-shirt, red shorts, underwear, toiletries and mismatched socks. No wallet. No credit card. No money.

The bag that they packed for me wasn't much better. No cool outfit. No wallet. No credit card. And no money.

We met the ladies for tennis, Larry in his King Kong T-shirt with red shorts and me in a similarly mismatched outfit. They laughed. We let them know we were still broke. No problem.

The tennis game, doubles, was fun and not too competitive. They invited us to join them for a picnic lunch and swim on their last day there, Sunday.

We arrived on a secluded beach, on the naval base, and unpacked the food and beverages. They decided to take a swim before eating. As soon the two young ladies took off their outerwear, displaying themselves in bikinis, it became clear that I had not been paying very close attention. They were both drop-dead gorgeous! (Disco, don't stare!)

So there I was, 48 hours after one of the most harrowing events of my 29 years of life, on a pristine sandy beach, warm turquoise water, deep clear blue sky, 72°F, palm trees, delicious fresh fruit, Puerto Rican rum, still alive and swimming with my best friend and two mermaids. Pinch me!!

"Life is good!"

We called our wives every day to keep them up-to-date on how we were doing and when we expected to be back home. We did not tell them about the nurses yet. No need to add any extra drama to our marriages. After all, we were both faithful. And there was little risk that Larry would get laid wearing that King Kong T-shirt!

When we got back home, Larry, an officer and a gentleman, offered to repay our debt by hand-delivering a check to the nurses. His wife, Susan, said,

"No way! Not without me!" She rode along as his Radar Intercept Officer. And in retrospect, I suppose it was a good idea...

Postscript:

US Navy accident records show that most air crews that attempted this same landing did not live to tell about it. I was extraordinarily fortunate to have a consummate, cool-headed professional like Larry Neal as my teammate. He would go on to become a successful F-14 Tomcat pilot, himself. I am eternally grateful that we lived through this event so we could tell this story to our grandchildren.

Chapter 8

Fighter Pilot of the Year

1978 - 1979

January 1978 - Update on my Astronaut Track: Two big goals down, and two to go. I graduated from the Naval Academy and acquired an MS in Aerospace Systems. At this point, I was working on the third big goal, distinguishing myself as a top fighter pilot. That will be needed in order to get to the fourth aspiration, the US Naval Test Pilot School (TPS).

Fighter Pilot of the Year Competition

In early 1977, I was not an above average nugget (new) fighter pilot, instead I received a "bad" performance evaluation from my first CO, Dick Wyman. Three months later, with the help of Sam Montgomery and my new CO, Drex Bradshaw, I was selected for Top Gun, where I excelled.

The next year, an opportunity loomed before me that I did not anticipate. I could be in the running for Fighter Pilot of the Year. Wasn't that exciting? What were the criteria? In wartime, the criteria were dependent on performance while getting shot at, whereas the criteria during peacetime consisted of executing mission scenarios, while being observed by experts. Those missions included intercepts of "enemy" airplanes, dog fighting, low level navigation, and delivering weapons on target.

VF-43, home-based with us at NAS Oceana, conducted the Fleet Fighter ACM Readiness Program (FFARP). This was primarily an evaluation of our ability to perform combat air patrol intercepts and air combat maneuvering (ACM), more commonly known as dogfighting.

Fighter Air Wing (FITWING) One, also co-located with us, conducted the remaining competitive exercises or COMPEXs. The compilation of all the scores of all the pilots and RIOs determined which squadron(s) would earn the Operational Readiness "E" for Excellence.

How did we do? VF-102 ranked #1 and earned an "E," and I ranked

"Number ONE among all Atlantic Fleet fighter pilots." Yippie!

How is it possible that I came out on top, with such tough competition? I credit Top Gun. Their instructors pushed me to my limits and motivated me to learn how to do the vertical reversal. They also taught me how to remember and debrief all the fights in 3-dimensions. That focused me on lessons learned and helped my teammates and me to improve.

Top Gun training was a series of contests. I compare those contests to a tennis tournament. Imagine if you were a tennis player and you spent five weeks competing against the best players and coaches in the world and then returned to a tournament in your hometown. Do you think you would do well? How about if you played doubles and your partner had the same training, too? That was my good fortune. I had the benefit of Top Gun trained Bill "Nips" Foster in my backseat.

At that point in time, nobody could beat me in a one-on-one dogfight in an A-4 Skyhawk, F-4 Phantom, F-14 Tomcat, or the F-5 Tiger. Outside of the competitive exercises, I also had the opportunity to fight against one of the US Air Force's best fighter pilots in their newest fighter, the F-15 Eagle. I won 10 out of 11 contests. The one match that I lost, I intentionally gave away by getting into a horizontal turning fight, just to see what he could do. The F-15 Eagle ate me up in a New York minute!

(All of the aircraft, cited above, had a better (tighter) turn radius than the F-4 Phantom. If you got into a flat, turning fight, each one of them could easily turn inside of the Phantom's circle and quickly bring guns or missiles to bear. The way you win a dogfight in the Phantom, is to keep it vertical where they cannot touch you.)

Another important criteria was flight hours. I accumulated more flight hours than any other Navy fighter pilot, one year, 1978.

My year's total was 327.2 hours, best in both the Atlantic and Pacific Fleets. (In that year, I also surpassed the minimum 1500 total flight hours I would need to apply to TPS.)

My global lead in flight time was a record for which I had many people to thank.

I could only fly that many hours if I had Phantoms to fly. We had 230 great maintenance men led by petty officers, division officers, and department head, Mike Matton. Together, they formed the best fighter squadron maintenance department in the world.

My wife, as you already know, was very supportive of my flying extra hours, including nights and weekends. And I had RIO friends, like Larry "Vert" Neal, who happily flew those extra flight hours with me.

What other things ran in my favor for a competition for Fighter Pilot of the Year? One was the so-called Top Gun trophy. Iceman's trophy was a Hollywood invention for the first Top Gun movie, but the prize in the real world was getting invited back as an instructor. I was lucky enough to be invited back to both Top Gun and VF-43. (I declined both because of my pursuit of Test Pilot School.)

We covered what it means to be a hero in peacetime, in the Chapter "Heroes." It is to save airplanes and lives. By January 7, 1978, I had already saved two aircraft and four lives. On that day came the most dramatic save of all, a landing in Puerto Rico with a missing wheel in the last chapter. It was a boost to my reputation, got mention in my fitness report.

The Fighter Pilot of the Year decision came from the desk of Commander Fighter Wing One, Captain Samuel Flynn. I got to know Sam Flynn early in 1978 when he asked me to be Master of Ceremonies (MC) for the annual fighter pilot ball, the Fighter Fling. That program is covered later in the Navy Culture chapter under the title, The Joker. I was invited to repeat as MC in June 1979.

In May, 1979, while preparing for the Fighter Fling repeat, Captain Flynn told me that I qualified as,

"Fighter Pilot of the Year, 1978!" Awesome! □□

But the public announcement would name an F-14 Tomcat pilot, instead. They wanted to be fair to the Tomcat community. They could not fly as many hours as us or yank 'n bank their aircraft like the good old reliable Phantom. The Tomcats still had issues with their engines. So the award alternated every other year between Phantoms and Tomcats. In 1977, an F-4 pilot got the award. In 1978 it was the Tomcat's turn for public recognition. I didn't care. I did not need the public recognition.

Jerry Werner

Phantom Fighter Pilot of the Year, 1978

Commanding Officer Endorsement

June 30, 1978

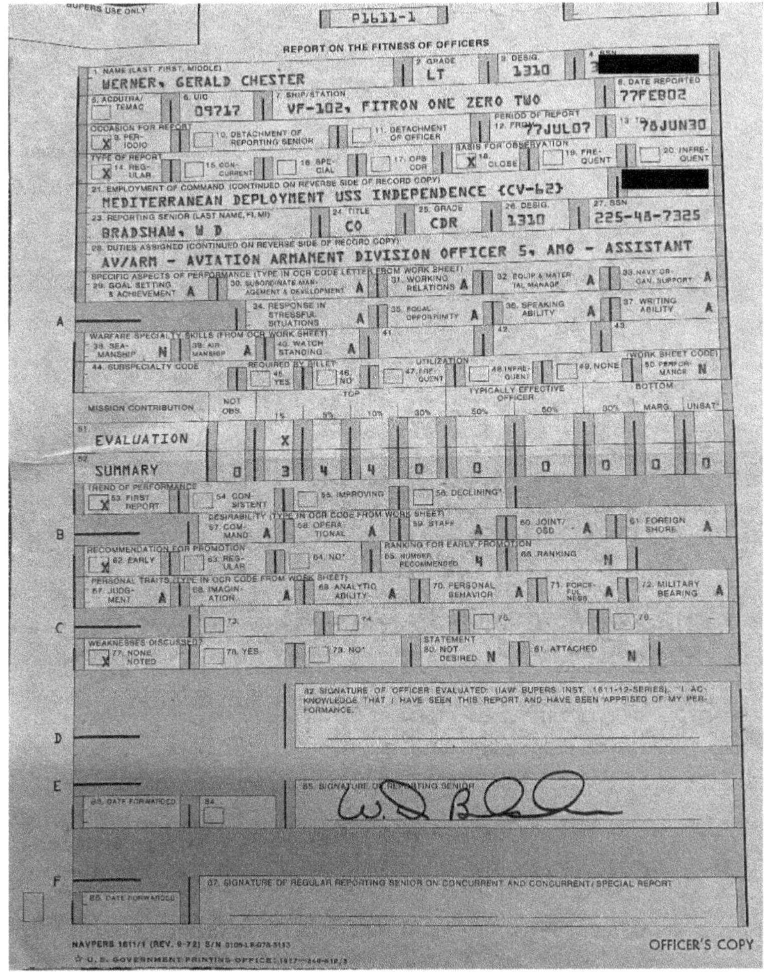

This was a key Fitness Report (Performance Evaluation) in my portfolio for requesting admission to the Test Pilot School.

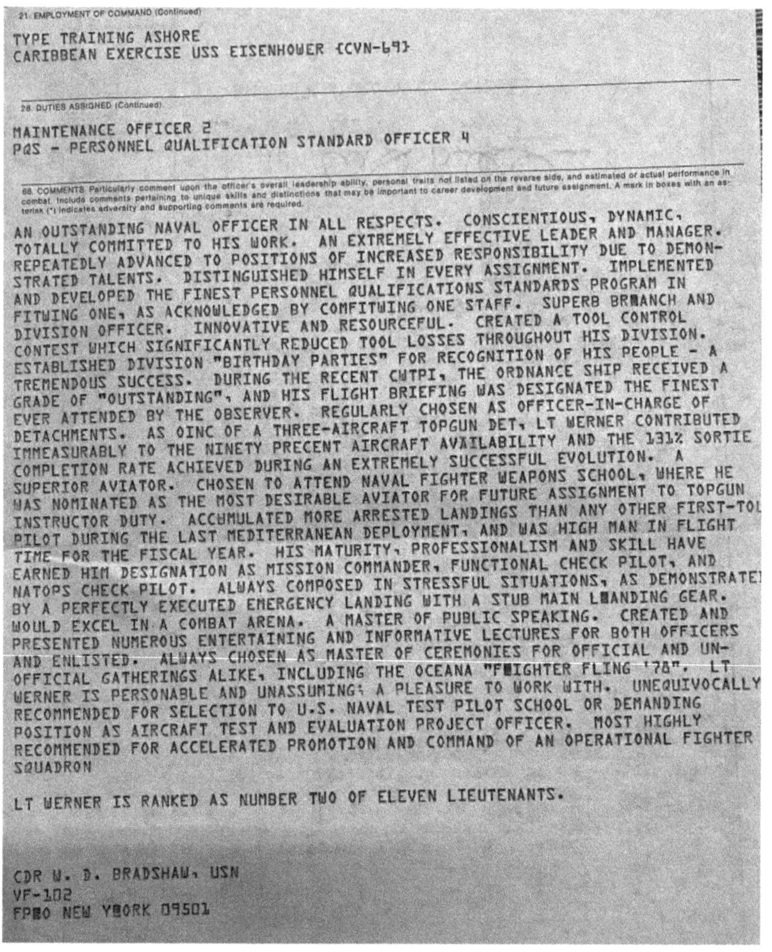

21. EMPLOYMENT OF COMMAND (Continued)

TYPE TRAINING ASHORE
CARIBBEAN EXERCISE USS EISENHOWER (CVN-69)

28. DUTIES ASSIGNED (Continued)

MAINTENANCE OFFICER 2
PQS - PERSONNEL QUALIFICATION STANDARD OFFICER 4

88. COMMENTS Particularly comment upon the officer's overall leadership ability, personal traits not listed on the reverse side, and estimated or actual performance in combat. Include comments pertaining to unique skills and distinctions that may be important to career development and future assignment. A mark in boxes with an asterisk (*) indicates adversity and supporting comments are required.

AN OUTSTANDING NAVAL OFFICER IN ALL RESPECTS. CONSCIENTIOUS, DYNAMIC, TOTALLY COMMITTED TO HIS WORK. AN EXTREMELY EFFECTIVE LEADER AND MANAGER. REPEATEDLY ADVANCED TO POSITIONS OF INCREASED RESPONSIBILITY DUE TO DEMONSTRATED TALENTS. DISTINGUISHED HIMSELF IN EVERY ASSIGNMENT. IMPLEMENTED AND DEVELOPED THE FINEST PERSONNEL QUALIFICATIONS STANDARDS PROGRAM IN FITWING ONE, AS ACKNOWLEDGED BY COMFITWING ONE STAFF. SUPERB BRANCH AND DIVISION OFFICER. INNOVATIVE AND RESOURCEFUL. CREATED A TOOL CONTROL CONTEST WHICH SIGNIFICANTLY REDUCED TOOL LOSSES THROUGHOUT HIS DIVISION. ESTABLISHED DIVISION "BIRTHDAY PARTIES" FOR RECOGNITION OF HIS PEOPLE - A TREMENDOUS SUCCESS. DURING THE RECENT CWTPI, THE ORDNANCE SHIP RECEIVED A GRADE OF "OUTSTANDING", AND HIS FLIGHT BRIEFING WAS DESIGNATED THE FINEST EVER ATTENDED BY THE OBSERVER. REGULARLY CHOSEN AS OFFICER-IN-CHARGE OF DETACHMENTS. AS OINC OF A THREE-AIRCRAFT TOPGUN DET, LT WERNER CONTRIBUTED IMMEASURABLY TO THE NINETY PRECENT AIRCRAFT AVAILABILITY AND THE 131% SORTIE COMPLETION RATE ACHIEVED DURING AN EXTREMELY SUCCESSFUL EVOLUTION. A SUPERIOR AVIATOR. CHOSEN TO ATTEND NAVAL FIGHTER WEAPONS SCHOOL, WHERE HE WAS NOMINATED AS THE MOST DESIRABLE AVIATOR FOR FUTURE ASSIGNMENT TO TOPGUN INSTRUCTOR DUTY. ACCUMULATED MORE ARRESTED LANDINGS THAN ANY OTHER FIRST-TOU PILOT DURING THE LAST MEDITERRANEAN DEPLOYMENT, AND WAS HIGH MAN IN FLIGHT TIME FOR THE FISCAL YEAR. HIS MATURITY, PROFESSIONALISM AND SKILL HAVE EARNED HIM DESIGNATION AS MISSION COMMANDER, FUNCTIONAL CHECK PILOT, AND NATOPS CHECK PILOT. ALWAYS COMPOSED IN STRESSFUL SITUATIONS, AS DEMONSTRATED BY A PERFECTLY EXECUTED EMERGENCY LANDING WITH A STUB MAIN LANDING GEAR. WOULD EXCEL IN A COMBAT ARENA. A MASTER OF PUBLIC SPEAKING. CREATED AND PRESENTED NUMEROUS ENTERTAINING AND INFORMATIVE LECTURES FOR BOTH OFFICERS AND ENLISTED. ALWAYS CHOSEN AS MASTER OF CEREMONIES FOR OFFICIAL AND UNOFFICIAL GATHERINGS ALIKE, INCLUDING THE OCEANA "FIGHTER FLING '78". LT WERNER IS PERSONABLE AND UNASSUMING; A PLEASURE TO WORK WITH. UNEQUIVOCALLY RECOMMENDED FOR SELECTION TO U.S. NAVAL TEST PILOT SCHOOL OR DEMANDING POSITION AS AIRCRAFT TEST AND EVALUATION PROJECT OFFICER. MOST HIGHLY RECOMMENDED FOR ACCELERATED PROMOTION AND COMMAND OF AN OPERATIONAL FIGHTER SQUADRON

LT WERNER IS RANKED AS NUMBER TWO OF ELEVEN LIEUTENANTS.

CDR W. D. BRADSHAW, USN
VF-102
FPO NEW YORK 09501

"An outstanding naval officer in all respects. Conscientious, dynamic, totally committed to his work. An extremely effective leader and manager. Repeatedly advanced to positions of increased responsibility due to demonstrated talents. Distinguished himself in every assignment.

Implemented and developed the finest Personal Qualification Standards (PQS) program in Fighter Wing One, as acknowledged by FITWING ONE staff.

Superb Branch and Division officer. Innovative and resourceful. Created a tool control contest which significantly reduced losses throughout his division. Established division "birthday parties" for recognition of his people. A tremendous success.

During the recent CWTPI, the ordnance ship received a grade of Outstanding, and his flight presentation was designated the finest ever attended by the observer.

Regularly chosen as officer-in-charge (OINC) of detachments. As OINC of the 3-aircraft TOPGUN DET, LT WERNER contributed immeasurably to the 90% aircraft availability and 131% sortie completion rate, achieved during an extremely successful evolution.

Superior aviator. Chosen to attend Naval Fighter Weapons School where he was nominated the most desirable aviator for future assignment to TOPGUN instructor duty.

Accumulated more arrested landings than any other first year pilot during the last Mediterranean deployment. Was high-man for fighter pilot flight time for the fiscal year (in the entire US Navy.)

His maturity, professionalism, and skill have earned him designation as Mission Commander, Functional Check Pilot, and NATOPS Check Pilot.

Always composed in stressful situations, as demonstrated by a perfectly executed emergency landing with a stub main landing gear. Would excel in a combat arena.

A master of public speaking. Created and presented numerous entertaining and informative lectures for both officers and enlisted. Always chosen as Master of Ceremonies for official and unofficial gatherings alike, including the Oceana Fighter Fling '78.

LT Werner is personable and unassuming. A pleasure to work with. Unequivocally recommended for selection to US Naval Test Pilot School or Test and Evaluation Project Officer.

Most highly recommended for accelerated promotion and command of an operational fighter squadron."

CDR W. D. Bradshaw, USN

30 June 1978

Special Attributes

I didn't realize till later in life that I was born with some attributes that were perfect for a fighter pilot. I already discussed my comfort with being upside down, in a spin or pulling Gs. In addition, my eyesight, body dimensions, composure during emergencies and lastly, an internal fuel gauge were all important assets.

Eyesight. At 20/10, I could identify an adversary aircraft at twice the distance of someone with normal vision. That meant that I could start taking aggressive actions much sooner than the other guy.

Body dimensions. Sometimes we can wish for two things that are mutually exclusive, like being a giant and being a fighter pilot. As a high school basketball player, I was up against a giant from Altoona High School named Greg. He stood a foot taller than me. I wanted to be Greg's height, but that would've made me too tall for an ejection seat and I could not have been a fighter pilot. My 5'9" frame, with a 6'1" wingspan, turned out to be absolutely perfect for the F-4 Phantom cockpit.

Composure during emergencies. My brothers and I witnessed a serious car accident at the Amy intersection where I grew up. A man was lying on the ground, badly injured from the collision. Only one adult was home, and that was the 30 year old mother of 4, across the street. She lost it and was running around her front yard like a chicken with its head cut off. (A common farmer's expression) At 12 years old, I was the one who checked in with the injured man and got on the phone for an ambulance.

One winter morning, while riding a yellow Elk Mound school bus up a steep icy hill, the bus started sliding backwards and the driver could not stop it. We slid off the road and plunged into a ravine backwards. The 24,000-pound bus came to rest on a small 4 inch diameter tree that prevented us from going all the way down the cliff. The bus stood almost vertical. The bus driver froze with his hands on the wheel and was not moving. I climbed down to the back of the bus, opened the rear emergency door and led the children out, including my little sister Barbie. The tree looked like it could give way at any moment. I heard cracking. I climbed to the front of the bus and asked the bus driver to come with me out the front door, near him. He finally let go of his grip on the steering wheel, and I helped him out to safety - in the nick of time. Just as he had both feet on the ground, that small tree broke off and the bus went tumbling a thousand feet down into the canyon and exploded in a massive fireball!!

(Just kidding! That little tree, miraculously held up, and everybody was OK.) I was 15 years old.

<u>Internal fuel gage</u>. Remember, the guy whom I met in the Officer's Club in Rota, Spain? He was being sent back home because he had three low fuel emergencies in the F-4. I made a mental note that I would have to pay close attention to fuel management. (The Phantom can gobble up its entire 4100 gallons of fuel in 15 minutes of full afterburner.) I don't know about other pilots, but I created a

living fuel gauge in my head and had a good idea of how much fuel I was burning at all times, even though my focus was outside the airplane, chasing down the bad guy. I "felt" when it was the right time to shut off the afterburners to preserve that resource. I would say it was similar to a microwave. When you use the 30 second warm-up button many times, you can develop the ability to guess pretty close to when 30 seconds will expire.

How do you achieve the top spot in a very competitive environment? I recently reviewed TV documentaries on sports stars Stephen Curry (NBA basketball, MVP Golden State Warriors), Michael Jordan (NBA basketball, MVP Chicago Bulls), and Tom Brady (NFL football, MVP New England Patriots). All of them experienced setbacks or rejection at one time or another. Stephen Curry was under rated most of his career. Michael Jordan was cut from his high school basketball team and, as a professional, broke his foot. Tom Brady could not secure the full-time quarterback position in college, was 199th in the NFL draft, and started it out as third string quarterback with the New England Patriots. All of them eventually achieved real stardom. You know my story, I experienced more than a dozen rejections or setbacks, before becoming Fighter Pilot of the Year.

Winners have many assets in common: Motivation, work ethic, discipline, mutual respect, physical fitness and an unwavering commitment to winning. They refuse to lose.

<u>Motivation</u>. Some people are motivated by the desire for approval from a parent or a role model. That was not the case for me. I was motivated by the desire to prove to the naysayers and the detractors that I could achieve the next step and stay on track for a trip to Mars.

<u>Work ethic</u>. There is a humorous TV ad using professional golfers bragging to one another how much earlier they get up in the morning to practice, than their opponent. The ultimate competitor never sleeps and practices all night long! Of course, that is an exaggeration for comedic purposes, but the leaders in all professional sports spend a lot more time working on their game than the average performer. Remember, when I was at Top Gun, Larry "Vert" Neal and I worked on mastering the vertical reversal, three days in a row, rather than going to happy hour. We never lost another one-on-one dogfight after that.

<u>Discipline</u>. My mother was really stressed when she learned that I had been chosen to fly jets for the Navy. I was so forgetful as a child that she made many trips to school with stuff that I had left behind, like my gym bag, text books and musical instruments.

Mom: "I worry about you Jerry, that you will forget something."

Jerry: "No Need to worry, Mom, we have checklists for everything."

Mom: "Well, Jerry, don't forget to do your checklists!"

I followed the safety rules and completed my checklists to the best of my ability. I regularly reviewed those immediate action emergency procedures that had to be memorized.

<u>Mutual respect</u>. I think mutual respect for both teammates and opponents is one of the reasons why Tom Brady was able to play in the NFL at quarterback for 20 years. When you show respect to your teammates, they protect you. When you show respect to your opponents, they tend to respect you in return. Most opponent rushers did not intentionally go after Tom Brady to try to hurt him.

<u>Physical fitness</u>. It goes without saying that the great sports superstars are in phenomenal physical shape. But Tom Brady took it several steps beyond, with diet and exercise, because of his desire to continue playing at high-level well into his 40s. Fighter pilots have to be prepared to go into their arena where the speeds are supersonic and the G forces 7.5+. At 7.5 G, a 150 lb. (68 kg) person weighs 1125 lb. (510 kg). It takes a toll on the body even when you are in really great physical condition. While I was a member of the squadron, there were 40 pilots and RIOs in VF-102, and only one of them smoked cigarettes.

<u>Refuse to lose</u>. I grew up very competitive. I loved to win and hated to lose. That certainly did not change when I became a fighter pilot.

They had a saying, "No points for second place!" and I lived by that. Whoever was flying on my wing or sitting in my backseat was my teammate. I would cheer them on and support them in every way. But if they weren't doing their job, they would hear from me. Even if the guy in my backseat was the big boss, the commanding officer, if he wasn't doing his job, I was screaming at him!

"Lock him up, goddamnit!" (Interpretation: Lock up the 'enemy' airplane on the radar so I could shoot a missile at him.)

Zoom Straight to Heaven

If I wasn't flying on Sunday mornings, at sea, I would usually attend Catholic Mass, on the aircraft carrier. So when the Catholic Chaplain, Father Kelley, wanted to go flying in an F-4 Phantom, I was an easy choice to be the pilot.

The priest had to go through all of the same requirements to ride in my backseat, as Sheila did in Meridian: Aviation physiology, in-flight emergency procedures, ejection seat training, cockpit familiarization, communication / coordination, and safety briefings.

It was February 25, 1978. We were the first Air Wing to conduct regular flight operations on the newest aircraft carrier, the USS Eisenhower (CV-69). It was our second month of operations. I was flying the Diamondback's F-4J Phantom, Tail Number 153900. I briefed Father Kelley, about the flight, in the ready room. I then led him up to the flight deck where the plane captain strapped him into the backseat. He was wearing an oxygen mask, and we made sure that his microphone was "hot" at all times. That was for safety reasons, so I could hear how he was doing and he didn't have to fumble with any switches in order to talk to me.

I went through all the pre-launch procedures and powered up my Phantom on the starboard catapult. The aircraft was shaking in full roaring afterburner. I saluted the catapult officer, he touched the deck, the man in the cat walk pushed the button and boom! Like a cannon shot, we raced from 0 to 180 knots (207 mph) in two seconds! The acceleration took his breath away, smashed his oxygen mask against his face and blurred his vision with eyeballs-in G!

Father Kelley yelled, "JESUS!"

I wasn't surprised.

I stayed in full afterburner at about 100 feet above the sea, and "cleaned up" the airplane, retracting the gear and flaps. I accelerated to about 600 knots and then pulled the pole back into my lap. The plane shot straight up, rocketing through 20,000 feet about 20 seconds.

Father Kelley screamed, "HOLY SHIT!"

That did surprise me…

I flew the rest of the mission in a more gentle manner. I did not want to make the man sick. After we returned to the carrier deck with an arrested landing, violent as it was, he was silent until he was sure that we had safely stopped, and then he said,

"AMEN!"

As a good parishioner, I responded, "Amen!"

Pushing the Edges of the Envelope.

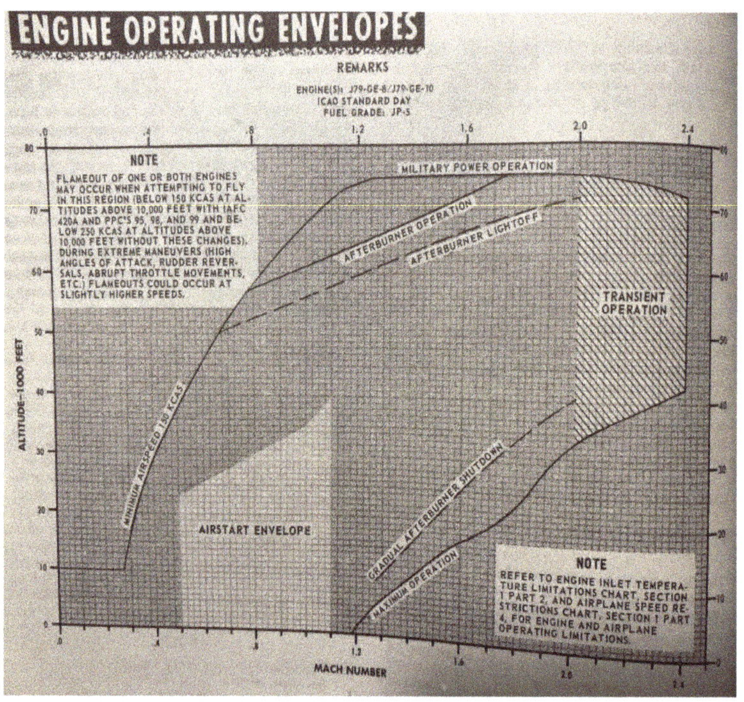

F-4J Phantom Engine Operating Envelopes

I know the picture above does not look much like an envelope, but the diagram of a simpler, slower airplane looks more like one. The engine operating envelope starts in the lower left corner of the picture with the airplane flying LOW and SLOW and progresses to the upper right hand corner, where the airplane is flying HIGH and FAST. The vertical scale is altitude in thousands of feet and the horizontal scale is Mach number, in fractions of the speed of sound.

A good fighter pilot has to explore all of the limits of the envelope and be able to safely control the aircraft, even at the extremes.

<u>Lower left</u>: The lowest altitude on the scale is zero, or sea level. The slowest speed, 150 knots.

<u>Upper right</u>: The highest altitude where the engines still run at military power, is 75,000 feet. And the fastest speed is between Mach 2.0 and Mach 2.4, called "Transient Operation," on the diagram. (Mach 2.0 = ~1534 mph)

While the highest altitude the F-4J was capable of reaching was 75,000 feet, we could not fly above 60,000 feet without a spacesuit. If you lost pressurization, up there, your blood would boil. We regular fighter pilots were not issued pressure suits, so 60,000 feet was our limit. My friends told me that at that altitude, the edge of space, they could see the curvature of the Earth and the sky looked more black than blue. So I gave it a try and zoomed up there. They were right. It was pretty cool! (Fortunately, I did not lose pressurization.)

You may remember my spending an entire solo flight, as a student in Pensacola, climbing to 40,000 feet so I could go fast downhill and break the sound barrier for the first time, in the TF-9 Cougar. That qualified me to wear the Mach 1.0 pin. (I ignored my friends, who were busting my balls about speedometer errors.)

There was also a Mach 2.0 pin available. I decided that I wanted one. I waited for a flight in an F-4J that did not have a centerline tank. That fuel tank limited our maximum speed to Mach 1.6. Without that tank, the aircraft was capable of speeds over Mach 2.2, so I decided to push that edge of the envelope.

I flew out to the military operating area off the coast of North Carolina called W-72. I flew parallel to the coast, about 50 miles away from land. In full afterburner, I climbed to 40,000 feet and did a series of camel humps to accelerate and continue to climb to 45,000 feet. From there I was already doing about Mach 1.8, I headed downhill in full afterburner. When you fly supersonic, every day, that speed is familiar and blasé. But as I approached 2X the speed of sound, with some low scattered clouds for reference, I noticed we were really haulin' ass!

The Mach Meter (speedometer) climbed, 1.85, 1.90, 1.95, 2.00, and then at 2.10 (~1600 mph)

WHAM!

The Starboard engine quit and we went into a wicked side skid! In a split second, I visualized a Hollywood cartwheel explosion streaming across the sky and my life flashed before my eyes! I pulled both throttles back to idle. The airplane straightened out, but the rapid deceleration threw me forward in my shoulder harness like an arrested landing that wouldn't quit. We slowed down from 1600 to 400 mph in just seconds! All the dirt in the cockpit, missing pencils, scraps of paper and dust bunnies went flying forward up on my dashboard! Whew!

As it turns out, the engine was fine. It quit because the sonic shockwave got sucked into the intake and cut off air to the engine. After we slowed down, the starboard engine came back to life. We had gone fast enough for my liking. I don't remember who my RIO was, but I'm sure he hasn't forgotten that flight either. And as for the Mach 2.0 pin, I don't ever remember wearing it. I didn't need a reminder of another near death experience.

MUSIC (Most requested at Werner's Party Central, 1977-1979)

- Staying Alive by The Bee Gees (Jerry "Disco" Werner's theme song for the remainder of his flying days in the Navy.)

- Other Songs by Andy Gibb and the Bee Gees

    - Shadow Dancing

    - Night Fever

    - How Deep is Your Love?

    - Love You Inside Out

    - (Our Love) Don't Throw It All Away

    - I Just Want to Be Your Everything

- Don't Leave Me This Way by Thelma Houston

- I'm Your Boogie Man by KC and the Sunshine Band

- Dancing Queen by ABBA

- You Make Me Feel like Dancing by Leo Sayer

- Margaritaville by Jimmy Buffett

- Hotel California by the Eagles

- Feels Like the First Time by Foreigner

- The Things We Do For Love by 10cc

- Handy Man by James Taylor

- Don't Stop by Fleetwood Mac

- Night Moves by Bob Seger and the Silver Bullet Band

- Heard It in a Love Song by the Marshall Tucker Band

- Carry On Wayward Son by Kansas

- Boogie Nights by Heatwave

- Go Your Own Way by Fleetwood Mac

- I Will Survive by Gloria Gaynor

- Hot Stuff by Donna Summer

- YMCA by Village People

- In the Navy by Village People

- The Gambler by Kenny Rogers

- We Are Family by Sister Sledge

- Sultans of Swing by Dire Straits

- You're the One That I Want by John Travolta and Olivia Newton-John

- Lay Down Sally by Eric Clapton

- We Will Rock You/We Are the Champions by Queen

- Last Dance by Donna Summer

- Don't It Make My Brown Eyes Blue by Crystal Gayle

- Copacabana by Barry Manilow

Note to grandchildren:

I wrote this book for you. As you have noticed it is a roller coaster ride with highs and lows. This chapter ends on a very high note, Fighter Pilot of the Year and an endorsement for Test Pilot School, but will it be enough to get me there? You will find out as you read on.

Chapter 9
The US Navy Culture (1966-1981)

Warning: Some readers may find content in this chapter objectionable. Not suitable for children.

Sexism

The US Navy was a male-dominated heterosexual culture the entire time I was a member. It was similar to other male-dominated cultures, such as the Marines, Army, and most police forces. Women were generally not treated as equals.

Women have served in the U.S. Navy since World War I, but naval aviation was not open to them until 1972. Shortly after the arrival of the first women aviation candidates, the Pensacola News Journal published an editorial cartoon that depicted a female fighter pilot sitting in the front seat of an F-4 Phantom. Long hair was flowing out the bottom of her helmet. She was pointing to the plane captain with long fingernails. The caption read: "I don't know what's wrong, but a noise comes out of the whatchamacallit whenever I press the thingamajig." I admit that I smiled. But that cartoon implied that women weren't technically smart enough to fly military airplanes and the Navy would let them pass anyway. Of course, neither was true, and it was not funny. It was a challenging time for the young women who joined us, as it is for all trail blazers.

Many sailors were oblivious to the inappropriate photographs they displayed. Pictures of naked women could be seen practically anywhere. Playboy Centerfolds not only adorned men's lockers, they were also sometimes posted on the wall, in public view. Slides of nudes were interspersed in pilot training programs. Called "treats," they were justified as a way of keeping the male audience alert during what might otherwise be a long, boring training session.

Happy hour at many officers' clubs featured topless women, dancing on tables or on the bar. During one happy hour in Meridian, Mississippi, my buddy Rick Robinson was flirting with one of the locals. She wanted his flight suit. He told her she could have it as long as she stripped naked. So she took off all of her clothes, handed them to him and put on his flight suit.

I described, in another chapter, the commanding officer who grabbed women's butts at parties. He was certainly not alone in that habit. It was clearly "sexual-harassment," but no one that I knew in the 1970s was disciplined for it. (It was not considered "sexual assault.")

As more and more women entered the Navy, in the 70s, most of them found the environment of nude women on display to be objectionable. Some women addressed it with leadership, but came away dissatisfied. The usual response was something like "Boys will be boys!" So one enlisted woman in VT-7 posted a picture of a nude man holding a watermelon from the centerfold of Playgirl magazine, on the wall behind her desk. The male pilots in the squadron were outraged! They ran to the skipper and demanded that she be ordered to take it down immediately. The Commanding Officer instead did the right thing and ordered the removal of all nude photos of both sexes in his squadron.

Treatment of women in the Navy finally came to a head in 1991 at the Tailhook convention in Las Vegas. That year became infamous for the incidents of sexual assault and harassment that took place. Here's an overview of what happened:

The Tailhook Association was an organization primarily composed of naval aviators who landed on aircraft carriers using a tailhook. Their annual symposium and convention were usually held in Las Vegas. In 1991, the convention took place at the Las Vegas Hilton Hotel.

The event attracted hundreds of Navy and Marine Corps officers and personnel every year gathered to socialize and participate in professional development activities. Some were veterans of Operation Desert Storm, the first Iraq war, which had concluded earlier in the year. By default, I was invited every year after I was aircraft carrier qualified. But I wasn't interested in Vegas gambling or raucous partying. I had more fun partying at home with my wife and friends.

The convention had a reputation as a setting where pervasive sexual misconduct occurred. Reports indicated that a significant number of attendees engaged in inappropriate behavior towards female attendees that year. This included groping, inappropriate touching, indecent exposure, verbal abuse, and even sexual assault. The incidents happened primarily within the hospitality suites, where heavy drinking was prevalent.

Notably, the misconduct occurred during what was known as the "gauntlet." This involved people lining the hallways of the hotel, where women were encouraged to walk through while being subjected to lewd and degrading behavior. 83 women and 7 men reported having been assaulted. What made 1991 different was that one of the women assaulted was 29 year old Lieutenant Paula Coughlin. She was a Naval aviator, victimized along with the others. She pressed charges, even though she knew it could cost her a Navy career.

During the investigations into the Tailhook scandal, several key findings emerged, widespread sexual misconduct, failure of leadership, victim blaming, lack of reporting and accountability, and inadequate training and policies.

As a result of the Tailhook scandal, according to Google's AI called Bard, the Tailhook Association settled out of court for $400,000. The Las Vegas Hilton was found negligent of providing adequate security for attendees and paid over $5 million in damages.

Fourteen admirals and nearly 300 naval aviator careers were damaged for their involvement in the misconduct, or their failure to address it appropriately. One of my favorite people was caught up in the wide sweep. He was nowhere near the convention and worked in the Office of the Secretary of the Navy. He was Captain Mike Matton, who I had expected would become an Admiral one day.

The scandal had several long-term effects on the US Navy and the military as a whole. There was a cultural shift, policy changes, increased awareness, improvements in reporting, increased accountability, and implementation of prevention programs. The Tailhook Convention was canceled in 1992. It has since been rebranded as Hook, a more respectable event.

In the wider Navy, nude photos were gone from lockers. Treats were gone from training programs. Dancing girls were gone from the Officer Clubs. Special happy hour pricing on drinks was eliminated. Leadership came down hard on men who appeared to have a drinking problem, giving some of them a choice to either leave the Navy or go to the Navy's version of Alcoholics

Anonymous. Reporting and discipline for sexual-harassment became a reality.

Coffee

Coffee? This might seem an odd subject to include in a chapter about U.S. Navy culture, but before you finish the book, you will understand.

When sailors weren't over-consuming alcoholic beverages ashore, they were often over-caffeinating with coffee on board the ship where it was free. But when shore based, coffee drinkers had to pay for their own. It was referred to as the Coffee Mess. Everybody in the squadron had to contribute a monthly fee to the Coffee Mess to keep the brew flowing. I was one of the few guys who did not drink coffee. I objected to the $5 monthly fee ($33 in 2023 dollars), starting with VT-9 in Meridian. I had varying degrees of success at getting out of paying for their coffee.

By the time I reached the USS Independence with VF-102, a new problem presented itself. We junior officers, in rotation, stood a day-long watch as the Squadron Duty Officer (SDO). It had serious responsibilities:

- Ensuring the readiness of the squadron's aircraft and personnel for flight operations.

- Supervising the squadron's flight operations.

- Handling any emergencies that may arise from flight operations.

- Maintaining the squadron's administrative records.

- Providing support to the squadron commanding officer and other squadron officers.

On top of all of this, when we had the duty, we were told to make coffee, whenever the pot was empty. I refused. I told the coffee drinkers to make their own coffee. I was too busy with serious duties.

That will come back to bite me.

Gays in the Navy

On an evening in 1977, I was doing a show on the aircraft carrier's radio station. I was playing popular music and reading what I could find on news, weather, and sports. Anita Bryant, the actress and singer, was in the news for organizing a protest against a Miami law protecting gay rights. At the same time, she was well known for her Florida orange juice commercials. I commented, on the air, that gays would probably retaliate by boycotting Florida orange juice.

The station manager rushed into the studio and gave me the "cut" signal. He said it was inappropriate for me to make any political comments, and that if I did it again, I would not be allowed to be a DJ at his radio station. I agreed with him. It was inappropriate. As it turns out, my prediction was also wrong. On the contrary, Anita Bryant was the one to lead a boycott of her employer, the Florida Citrus Growers Association, because they did not support her efforts to deny gays equal rights to housing and employment.

The radio station manager and his assistant may have been gay. 1977 was still a very difficult time to be an American gay man, especially in the U.S. Navy. If you admitted to or were found to be homosexual, you were automatically dismissed. It was not until 1991, when Bill Clinton was President, that gays were allowed to serve in the military, as long as they followed the rule, "Don't ask. Don't tell."

The restrictions on non-heterosexual members ended under President Barack Obama's administration in 2011. Same-sex marriage was recognized in all 50 US States in 2015.

The Joker

I was better known as a comedian than as a top fighter pilot. How did that happen?

I remember a talent show in the basement of Saint Joseph's Church, when I was in the fifth grade. I told a few jokes and the audience, made up of mostly adults sitting in folding chairs, erupted in laughter. Apparently, I had the ability to make people smile.

Where did that come from? Perhaps from my dad, who was always exercising situational humor. There was a shaggy headed boy in the neighborhood named Buddy Woolford. Dad called him Wooly Buddford. One of my shy childhood friends was Denny Stahlbush. Dad called him Stawly Denbush. There was a popular western TV show, at the time, called "Bat Masterson." He referred to the show as Matt Basterson, to which my mother yelled from the other room, "Don't you be swearing in front of the kids!"

During my senior year of high school, I went to Wisconsin Boys State, where we learned about local and state government. Most of the boys focused on getting elected to office as mayor or governor. I tried out for Master of Ceremonies for the talent show. I got the job.

I studied a couple of books of jokes. They were mostly bad jokes. On the night of the show, 1000 people showed up. It was my job to kick off the show, introduce each of the acts, and do a closing. I found out early that I got some great audience reactions to jokes that were based on bad puns. I really got the crowd going to the point where they were trying to boo me off the stage.

1. Why did the scarecrow win an award? Because he was outstanding in his field!
2. What do you call a lazy kangaroo? Pouch potato!

Why did the bicycle fall over? Because it was too tired!

"Get the hook!" They yelled. The more they booed, the more I subjected them to bad puns! Ha ha ha!

As you read earlier, while I was at the Naval Academy, I organized a folk group called the Anchormen. I was the spokesman for the group and introduced the songs and told a few jokes between numbers. We did as many as five shows a day for a week on tour. I learned that a specific joke, told in exactly the same way to two different audiences, could get quite different responses. Some thought my joke was hilarious, and others didn't think it was funny at all. Each audience was different.

One of the reasons my USNA academics were really a struggle one semester was because I wrote the radio comedy series called "The Adventures of YP 654". It was very popular, but incredibly time-consuming.

When I got to a squadron, I learned about "Hail and Farewell" parties. The typical tour of duty, at a squadron, was three years. That meant that pretty much every month, one person was leaving, and a new person was arriving to replace them. The senior guys would always have a few words to say about the guy who is leaving, mostly complimentary.

I started doing stand-up comedy at Hail and Farewell parties at VT-9 in Meridian. They happened every month or two and wives and girlfriends were also invited. I usually "roasted" the guys who were leaving and ribbed some other individuals in the room. (A "roast" is a form of humor, in which a specific individual, a guest of honor, is subjected to jokes at their expense.) I also "read" answers to questions, sealed in envelopes, similar to Johnny Carson's Carnac the Magnificent. My humor was a hit with most of the participants.

When I was the FRAMP officer in Virginia Beach, Speedy Seay asked me to create a farewell video for the outgoing VF-101 Skipper, JD Disher. He was one of the good guys, so that made it easier to do. But it surprised me how much time it took to weave together still photos and video clips with my narration voice. It took 10 hours in the studio, with the help of professionals, to record just 10 minutes of video. Captain Disher loved it and thanked me in person.

Before my first VF-102 Commanding Officer, Dick Wyman, left, we had a farewell party for him. I imitated him as a little league baseball coach. I dressed the part with a baseball cap, aviator sunglasses, T-shirt, jeans and a little beer belly. I delivered a lecture titled, "Get Your Head Screwed on Right About Baseball!" Of course all of the little leaguers I was lecturing were aviators in his squadron. It was my chance to pick on them, too. Dick was a good sport about it and so were they.

I think my best creation of all was "The Diamondback Tapes." I produced this audio tape for our goodbyes to my second VF-102 Commanding Officer, Drex "Goober" Bradshaw. It was a 20 minute production that used clips from popular songs to match the antics or personality of each of the pilots and RIOs in the squadron. Their wives and girlfriends also got mentioned, including mine. It was very popular. I made a bunch of copies for those who wanted it.

As a result of my reputation with the Diamondbacks, I was invited to do a standup routine for the Air Wing's at-sea-entertainment forum, called the Fo'c's'le Follies. It took place in the forward part of the aircraft carrier, below the flight deck. In the days of Columbus, ships were fitted with castle-like structures fore and aft. The structures have disappeared, but the term forecastle remains. And on the USS Eisenhower the forecastle was big enough for 200 guys to attend the show.

I performed at three Fo'c's'le Follies. At the first one, I roasted the captain of the ship. In the second show, I roasted the admiral. During all three of them, I made jokes about the commanding officers of the squadrons and other worthy characters.

MEMORANDUM

From: CVW-7 ASW OPS
To: Squadron XO's/Talent Coordinator

Subj: FO'C'S'LE FOLLIES

1. Intend to present the second FO'C'S'LE FOLLIES/Award Night on Sunday, 24 July 1977 during our Kithira Anchorage.

2. Plan on having a meeting with squadron coordinators, 16 July (time to be announced).

Very respectfully,

W. W. KENNEDY
LCDR, USN

At my final performance, I may have crossed a line. While waiting in the queue for a meal at the officer's mess, I picked up a lot of gossip. The VF-33 Executive Officer appeared to be guilty of hypocrisy, as he demanded that all of his aviators purchase and wear a yellow VF-33 T-shirt, while he himself did not wear one. They were even subject to discipline if they did not.

In my presentation to the audience, I added: "Your XO looks like a cheapskate. We sympathize with you guys, we don't like him much either."

That one line triggered a hostile response from him at about 2 AM. He roused all of his junior officers from their sleep, and ordered them to gather in the ready room. When they were all assembled, he read them the riot act. Obviously, I wasn't there, so I don't know what was really said, but I was told that he defended his failure to purchase and wear the required T-shirt because he had serious financial problems at home. However, his main grievance was his junior officers talking about him behind his back.

His boss, the VF-33 Commanding Officer, heard about the XO's outrageous behavior the next morning. Two days later, the VF-33 XO was gone from the ship. Did I cross a line, or did he? Do we want a man leading a fighter squadron who can't take a joke?

As mentioned earlier in this chapter, I was invited to be Master of Ceremonies for the annual fighter pilot's ball called the Fighter Fling, 1978, by the Commander Fighter Wing One, Captain Sam Flynn. It was a formal affair with all of the East Coast Naval aviators wearing their formal dress white uniforms and the ladies in long gowns, about 700 people, at the Omni Hotel in Virginia Beach.

My wife, Christine and I sat at the head table. As MC, I did the opening, introductions, and closing. In between, I did my own little comedy routine. The premise of the skit was that Captain Sam Flynn was so old that he was a member of the first Carrier Qualification class with hot air balloons. Instead of meatball, lineup, and angle of attack, they focused on meatball, lineup, sand, and gas. The routine included jokes about several of the commanding officers who were in the room. The crowd loved it. Sam loved it. I got invited back.

As the Master of Ceremonies for the Fighter Fling in the second year, 1979, I was informed that the Chief of Naval Operations (CNO), Admiral Thomas Hayward, would be at the head table with my wife and me. He was the CEO of the US Navy. Captain Flynn told me that I could not use any curse words in front of the CNO. That would be difficult since my script was already written, so I bought a bicycle horn, the kind with the squeezable air bulb. I used it to bleep out any offending words.

I invited a guest of honor, Randy "Duke" Cunningham, the Vietnam War Ace and former Top Gun instructor. Like so many fighter pilots, he had the kind of prominent personality type that made him easy to roast. The premise of the 10 minute presentation was that the Duke never got enough credit for his accomplishments. No matter what he did, even shooting down five enemy MiGs, "There were no dancing girls, no cheering crowds, or confetti." It was my finest hour for stand-up comedy. Randy was laughing so hard he cried. And again, the crowd loved it!

Before I move on, I need to say that humor was my way of showing respect for people. Perhaps a little too much, at times. But they will have a chance to get even with me, coming up.

They Even the Score

I heard all about aviator bachelor parties, while I was stationed in Pensacola; heavy drinking, porn on the TV, prostitutes and general debauchery. There were stories about guys stripping the bachelor naked and locking him in a closet with a naked hooker. They also did the same to other people, like the father of the bride. I was not interested. I was invited to a couple of parties and declined. Nobody even suggested organizing a bachelor party for me.

Against that background, seven years later, my good buddy Russ "Craze" Plappert invited me to his bachelor party. I asked if there were going to be any hookers attending. Russ said he didn't think so, but I should ask the organizer. I talked to him and he assured me that there would be no prostitutes. He said there would be pornography playing on the TV in the living room, but I could easily avoid that. I wasn't that much of a prude, I just didn't want to get squeezed into a closet with a working girl and have to explain that to my wife.

The bachelor party was held at one of the junior officers' homes. I arrived on time and found just about all of the officers in the squadron there, except the Skipper and XO. The beer was flowing, and the porn was playing in the living room as advertised.

About a half hour later, somebody announced that the party was about to get started. I was directed to a seat, facing the front door in a big comfy padded chair. The doorbell rang. One of the guys went outside to talk to the visitor. A few minutes later a pretty young lady comes through the door. In less than 30 seconds, she strips off all of her clothes, leaving them in a pile at her feet, without any attempt to do a striptease. She had a laser-like focus on me, walked over, climbed up and sat on my shoulders, straddling the back of my head. She began gyrating.

My face must've turned three shades of RED. The guys gave her a standing ovation. What a scene! Some were rolling on the floor laughing. Some must have peed themselves! They were hilariously entertained that Jerry "Disco" Werner finally got his due!

I was a good sport about it. I let her finish what she had been paid to do. Then she climbed down to entertain others. I remained at the party for another half hour or so, but was not going to press my luck, just in case they had something else in mind. I excused myself and headed home, where I immediately took a shower…

After all the roastings and jokes I had aimed at my squadron mates, over the years, they finally got even!

Note to Grandchildren:

Regarding my role as The Joker, I should've been more considerate of other people's feelings. The best humor is self deprecating, making fun of oneself. One of today's popular comedians who is very good at that is Jim Gaffigan.

I definitely crossed that line when I criticized our sister squadron's executive officer at the Follies. On the other hand, I may have done the Navy a favor by exposing someone who was not completely fit to be a commanding officer.

They Even the Score: After picking on my Diamondback teammates for three years, they found a way to get back at me. What goes around, comes around!

Gays in the Navy: I just want you to know that whoever you choose as your love partner and whatever you choose as your gender identity, I will love you and accept you, regardless. By saying that, this book may be banned in Florida and Texas, but I don't care. I didn't write this book for politicians. I wrote it for you.

Chapter 10
Test Pilot School and a Daunting Dilemma, 1979-1980

The roller coaster ride continues. The story picks up after the chapter entitled "Fighter Pilot of the Year." In that chapter, my commanding officer, Drex "Goober" Bradshaw, gave me a great fitness report (performance evaluation) documenting that I was number one at Top Gun, in first place in all of the competitive exercises, tops in flight hours, and had the most aircraft carrier landings among first tour pilots. His report also, importantly, included an endorsement for Test Pilot School.

CDR Drexel Bradshaw, 1979

The significance of all of this was that I finally achieved my third big goal, to be recognized as a top fighter pilot. The last of the big four goals was to graduate from the test pilot school.

But Commander Bradshaw's fitness report would not be enough to propel me into TPS. I would need to submit a formal application and receive a strong endorsement from the Executive Officer, who was about to become my new Commanding Officer. He was a TPS graduate, CDR Bill "Snake" Denning. That package would then go to the Test Pilot School Selection Committee.

I needed to find someone to help me with my application. A buddy recommended CDR Stuart Fitrell, the commanding officer of one of our Airwing's A-7 squadrons, VA-66. He told me that Stu Fitrell was not only a very bright Naval Academy guy with a master's degree from Oxford, but he was also a test pilot and an astronaut finalist.

CDR Fitrell was always friendly towards me when we met or passed on the ship. He knew me from my missing wheel landing and my forecastle follies standup routine. So, when I approached him to ask for his advice, he enthusiastically agreed to meet.

Stu Fitrell gave me excellent advice about what to include in my application, what to emphasize, and how to present it. I took copious notes and followed his advice to the letter. (What neither of us knew at the time was that he would be on the Test Pilot School Selection Committee and would be presenting my case.)

The professional roller coaster ride would have one more high and one more low before the Test Pilot School Selection Committee met. The high point was my landing successfully with a broken tail. (See Heroes chapter) And the low point was my nearly killing my Commanding Officer, Bill Denning. (See Nightmare Catapult Shot chapter.) Would either of them be a factor?

Special Projects

To improve my odds for selection to the US Naval Test Pilot School, I took on three special projects: **Defeating Surface to Air Missiles (SAMS), Evaluation of the VTAS Helmet, and Using the Phantom Eye.**

Defeating Surface to Air Missiles (SAMS)

I presented to the squadron pilots the latest research on defeating surface to air missiles. The general rule of thumb was that if you could see the missile and had enough speed and separation, you could easily defeat it by making a dogfighting move. The comparative wing size makes it easy for an aircraft, with its much larger wings, to outturn a missile with its tiny wings, but you have to keep up your speed and execute sufficiently hard turns.

In addition, we were directed to use decoys, both chaff and flares, as demonstrated in the movie Top Gun: Maverick. The chaff (glass silicate fibers with an aluminum coating) can fool radar guided missiles while the flares attract heat seeking missiles away from the fighter.

The general rule of thumb for the F-4 Phantom was to maintain a minimum airspeed of around 500 knots and pull 4-5 g's in an unpredictable pattern. I described the practice routine that I used.

Finally, I told them that we should avoid a hostile SAM environment altogether, unless we had minimum visibility of 5 miles and minimum distance between cloud layers of 12,000 feet.

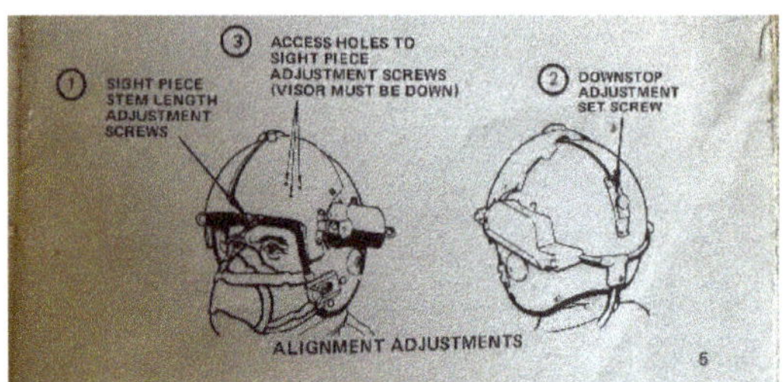

Evaluation of the VTAS Helmet

I evaluated the latest technology, Honeywell's Visual Target Acquisition System (VTAS) helmet. It was a precursor to today's very expensive helmets, worn by fighter pilots in single seat airplanes. It had electronics that connected the helmet to the airplane's radar system, so the radar would look where the pilot was looking and the radar image would appear on the inside of the pilot's visor. With a turn of his head, the pilot could look at the enemy aircraft, lock up the radar on the target and fire a missile at it.

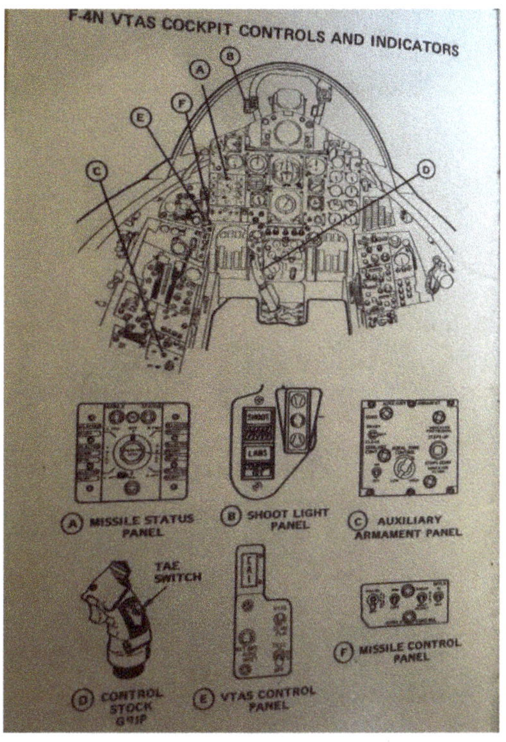

I gave VTAS passing grades, but it was heavy and clumsy. I would not want to wear that helmet in an actual dogfight. Under high g-forces, my head would be down in my lap!

Use of the Phantom Eye

The Phantom Eye was a telescope I mounted in the cockpit, aligned with the radar, that gave the pilot the ability to identify an enemy aircraft at great distance so he could fire a radar guided missile head on. This invention could have revolutionized tactics.

When a war begins, the so-called good guys are all on one side of the line and the bad guys on the other. It's clear at that point who is the enemy and who is not, but after the initial pass, all bets are off. You need to know who you're about to shoot down. What tactics did we use to accomplish that? Beginning during the Vietnam War, the leader of a team of two F-4 Phantoms, called a section, was required to fly close to the bogey to positively identify it as a friend or foe. The wingman, about a mile abreast, maneuvered into position to fire, if it turned out to be an enemy. These Visual ID tactics did not allow us to use our head-on weapon, before we ever engaged. It also tied up half the team just to identify the bogey rather than attacking an enemy.

The idea to mount a telescope in the cockpit came from an F-14 Tomcat pilot, who did it in a special exercise in the desert. He strapped a telescope in place with Velcro. He was able to ID even the tiniest fighter, the F-5 Tiger, at a great enough distance to use a head-on weapon against him. He called his invention, the Tomcat Integrated Telescope System (TITS). (Leave it to a fighter pilot to make it sexual…)

In the F-4 Phantom, I did not want to use Velcro. I wanted to make it a more permanent installation that could handle the rigors of aircraft carrier landings and dogfighting. I used small aluminum brackets fashioned in a metal working shop. I experimented until I found a configuration that worked. The telescope was aligned to the radarscope center bull's-eye, known as boresighting.

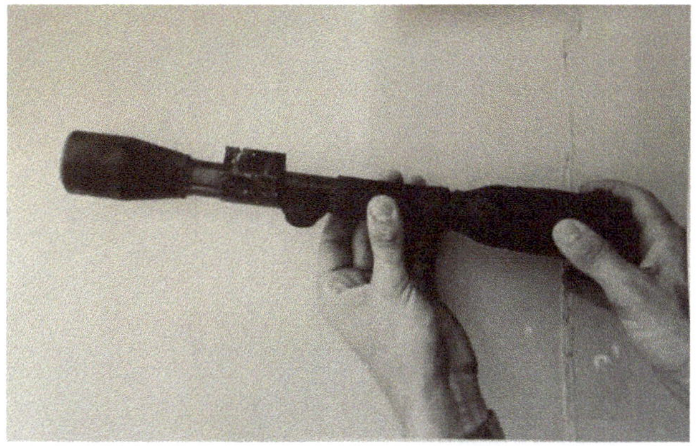

The new Phantom Eye procedure called for finding the bogey on the radar, aligning the aircraft so the target was in the middle of the radar screen, looking through the telescope to ID the airplane and shooting a Sparrow radar-guided missile head-on. If we could not get a radar lock to use the Sparrow, we could also fire the newest heat seeking missile, the AIM-9L Sidewinder, head-on as well.

Most of my buddies in VF-102 liked the idea and gave it a try. The new executive officer was an exception. CDR Dan "Lurch" Bunting claimed that it wasn't gentlemanly to shoot somebody in the face. The proper thing was to engage in a dog fight, and let the best man win. I didn't argue with him.

The Phantom Eye project was done under a special Navy program called Rapid Action Minor Engineering Change (RAMEC). That program was supposed to grant approval within 90 days, complete with blueprints and procedures for expanding it to other airplanes. But it took them more than a year. By then, F-4s were scheduled to be replaced by the F-14 Tomcat, so the project never got implemented. A similar installation could have been used on the F-14, but the Tomcat was scheduled to get an electronic system called Television Camera System (TCS). The Phantom Eye telescope installation cost about $250. TCS cost about $250,000. But TCS had more powerful amplification, worked together with the radar, and provided video recordings of encounters.

CDR Bill Denning

Commanding Officer Endorsement for Test Pilot School

Commander William J. Denning was the man I was counting on to give me a strong endorsement for the US Naval Test Pilot School. He was a graduate. He was my primary RIO for three months. We made a good team, even though I found myself, in the heat of competition, yelling at him to help us win the fight. It was the unique nature of Navy fighter crews in combat. We were all equals. We were all going to win and survive or we were going to lose and die. Death was not an option for me. But my last flight with him was as close to death as you can get. (Nightmare Catapult Shot.)

CDR Denning convened his department heads for the sole purpose of discussing my application to test pilot school. I was told later, by one of the participants, that the majority of department heads were very supportive of my application, but one person was dead set against it. He had failed to get into Test Pilot School himself. He said that because Werner would not make coffee when he was the Squadron Duty Officer that he was not a team player, and should not be recommended for TPS. Fortunately, for me, the other department heads disagreed. The "Yays" carried the day. It did make me second-guess my anti-coffee campaign, though.

Bill Denning sent a strong endorsement to the US Naval Test Pilot School Selection Committee. His submission included the fact that I was number one in just about everything and that my invention of the Phantom Eye could have serious implications for tactics. I would have to wait on their decision.

The Challenges of Marriage in the Navy

In the meantime, while waiting on the selection committee to make its decision, let's talk about marriage. In the earlier chapters, I had set aside a section called Romance. That disappeared after I got married. It's not that there was no romance at all, it was rare and fleeting. That was pretty normal for an established marriage. Remember, we got married in 1973, as newlyweds we had a 17 year-old living with us and we split our time between Pensacola and Meridian. We moved to Virginia Beach in December 1975. Our third wedding anniversary, May 26, 1976, I was hiding from the enemy, curled up in a flooded foxhole, freezing my ass off. The following February, I was on my way to the Mediterranean for a six month cruise. We missed our connection in Lucerne, Switzerland. We got one week together in Italy, but she had Mama with her. Get the picture?

We reconnected with our friends, Mike and Norma French, in Virginia Beach. Mike, as you will recall, was my Naval Academy classmate. Norma and Christine were both school teachers. All four of us read the book "Open Marriage," written by Nina and George O'Neill. Due to the high failure rate of traditional marriages, "Open Marriage" explores the concept of non-monogamous relationships and challenges established norms of marriage. The book ignited a significant cultural conversation at the time.

We all agreed with the Open Marriage recommendation that we not be tied to traditional roles, but we were not open to sex outside of marriage. Traditional roles? At that time, men were expected to deal with everything involving the automobile, grill meat on the barbecue, take out the trash, mow the lawn, pay the bills and fix anything that broke. The woman was expected to do all the cooking, cleaning, shopping, interior design, and child rearing. This was not possible in a Navy marriage. With the husband gone to sea, the wife was responsible for it all. When at home, we agreed that he should help her out with her traditional roles.

Regarding relationships with members of the opposite sex, outside of marriage, we all agreed that openness and honesty were essential. For example, if there was a movie in the theaters that Norma and I wanted to watch and Mike and Chris did not, we should be able to go to the movie together without any jealousy. Mike and Chris should feel free to do something else. We agreed that meals together, dancing, and theater were acceptable activities outside the marriage. We all drew the line at having sex with somebody else. In retrospect, we should've drawn the line at kissing on the lips. Men did not interpret that act as seriously as women did.

Chris and I agreed to have children before we married. I said I wanted a big family. She said okay, but not too big. In 1979, we found ourselves in the sixth year of marriage without seriously addressing the issue of children. We were still in party mode. By then, both of us realized the challenges of sea duty and family separation. We had just been informed by the Navy's leadership that, due to a shortage of pilots in my year group, we could expect back-to-back sea duty. I could be at sea for 12 straight months.

Chris threatened to go back home to Connecticut and end the marriage, rather than raising the children all on her own. I very much wanted to be involved with our kids, as much as possible. So we agreed that if I did not get into test pilot school, I would get out of the Navy and find another job where I could be home with the family. (We assumed that a career at NASA would have little family separation, except while on a space flight.)

She stopped taking birth control pills and got pregnant soon after. That was really exciting for both of us. But all of a sudden, I felt a big responsibility as an expectant father. I immediately started working on becoming a better role model. I focused on eliminating as much of the salty navy language as possible. After all, the fetus could hear me cursing, right?

All of a Sudden, It Becomes Possible

On June 1, I was notified that I was selected for the US Naval Test Pilot School class beginning July 16, 1979.

I was stoked!

My immediate thought was, when I graduate from the test pilot school, I will have met the minimum entrance requirements for NASA. I received congratulations from everybody I knew, especially heartfelt from my teammates in VF-102. I thanked everybody who made it possible, with special appreciation to Drew Bradshaw, Bill Denning, Larry Neal and Sam Montgomery. I also thanked Mom and Dad and Father Crowley. And, of course, I celebrated with my wife, Chris, who had been incredibly supportive all along.

Next, I received a congratulatory phone call from someone I was not expecting, CDR Stuart Fitrell. Remember him? He was the VA-66 Commanding Officer and astronaut finalist, who gave me excellent guidance on my application. As it turns out, he was drafted to the Test Pilot School Selection Committee, where he went to bat for me. I expressed my gratitude.

Another surprise, Fitrell had returned to the Patuxent River Test Center, where he would be the Head of the Ordnance Branch. He was living in a big new house in the woods, in Mechanicsville, Maryland, 45 minutes north of the test center. He invited Chris and me to dinner with his wife, Lynn, and their three children. He told us that we could get a lot more for our housing money in their neighborhood, rather than living close to the test center in Lexington Park. He offered to help us work with the contractor who built their home. That way we could carpool to the test center.

It all sounded good to us. Using his contractor, we built a very nice brick split-level home, four bedrooms, 2.5 baths, 2.5 car garage with a workshop. It was in the woods on a third of an acre. We had a patio and a fireplace. It was very peaceful. We had very few neighbors.

Our new baby was due around January 1. We took long walks every day. A stray dog followed us, but kept his distance. He was a medium sized, short-haired, mixed breed with floppy ears. With each subsequent walk, he got a little closer. Chris brought treats for him. She would leave a trail. He ate them all. He had survived for months on food left for him by the homebuilders. He lived with the deer. He bounded through the woods, just like them, snapping his tail up, showing the white on the bottom. Gradually day after day, he got closer and closer to Chris until he finally took a treat from her hand. I then knew that we had our new pet. He was my first dog. We named him Pooch and he became my best friend for the next 12 years.

Test Pilot School Curriculum

When I arrived at NAS Patuxent River, Maryland, I felt right at home. I had imagined this day for nearly 20 years. The US Naval Test Pilot School is known for being the best. Its comprehensive curriculum prepares students, very well, for the challenging role of a test pilot.

What is a test pilot? A test pilot's role is to fly new and modified aircraft to evaluate performance and safety features. Job duties include gathering observational data during test flights, documenting whether an aircraft is operating properly, and making recommendations for improvements. The Navy test pilot signs off on the new or improved aircraft, on behalf of the Navy. Regular pilots cannot fly the aircraft until it is cleared by the test pilot.

The curriculum covered a wide range of subjects and practical training. Here is an overview of some of the key areas covered in the program:

1. Flight Sciences: This included aerodynamics, flight mechanics, stability, and control.

2. Performance Analysis: Students learned about aircraft performance, including climb, endurance, range, and maneuverability.

3. Systems: This covered the various systems present in an aircraft, such as avionics, engines, hydraulics, and electrical systems.

4. Test Techniques: Students learned about the methodologies and techniques employed in flight testing, including planning, instrumentation, data collection, and analysis.

5. Test Management: This included test planning, risk assessment, safety procedures, and project management principles.

6. Human Factors: Students studied human performance and limitations, including cockpit design, crew resource management, and human-machine interfaces.

7. Aerospace Vehicle Systems: This involved understanding the different types of aircraft and their respective systems, such as fixed-wing aircraft, rotary-wing aircraft, and unmanned aerial systems (UAS).

8. Test Conduct: Students gained practical experience in flight testing in actual aircraft that exhibit characteristics being studied in the classroom. This included conducting test flights, evaluating performance, assessing aircraft parameters and submitting a professional report.

If you are a pilot and you love to fly a variety of aircraft, I can't think of a better place to be than at the US Naval Test Pilot School. Imagine that for one whole year your job is to fly every day supersonic, subsonic, taildraggers, jets, propellers, multi-engine, helicopters, gliders, World War II bombers, and commercial airliners! We would usually be in the classroom in the morning and flying in the afternoon. And our flights would often match what we were learning from the books. It was exhilarating!

I flew 13 different airplanes at TPS. Our motto was, "Show me how to start it and I'll fly it!"

1. North American T-2C Buckeye, twin-engine, subsonic jet

2. Northrop T-38A Talon, twin-engine, supersonic jet

3. Martin Marietta B-26 Marauder, twin propeller

4. Bell OH-58 Kiowa, single-engine helicopter

5. Douglas TA-4J Skyhawk, single-engine subsonic jet

6. Grumman OV-1B Mohawk, twin engine propeller

7. Bell AH-1G Cobra, single-engine, attack helicopter

8. Lockheed P-3B Orion, 4 propeller, anti-submarine

9. De Havilland U-6A Beaver, single prop, tail dragger

10. North American NT-33 T-Bird, twin-engine, subsonic jet

11. Scaled Composites X-26A Glider, no engine, very slow

12. Vought F-8J Crusader, single engine, supersonic jet

13. De Havilland NU-1B Otter, single prop, taildragger

Major Ed Traasdahl, USMC, was a classmate and became a friend. He had never flown in a supersonic aircraft before, so I took him up in the T-38 Talon and let him do most of the flying. I had never flown a helicopter before, so he took me up in the AH-1G Huey Cobra and let me do most of the flying. With his coaching, I learned how to take off, cruise, and land. The most challenging was landing because it required slowing down to zero air speed! Ouch! All I had ever flown were fixed wing airplanes where, for all those years, my focus was on keeping my speed fast enough so the airplane didn't stall. To slow to zero knots at first was scary. When I got used to it, it became fun. I also found flying sideways and backwards to be amazing.

Eventually, Ed let me try a simulated engine out landing. That's when you reduce the engine to idle and use the momentum from the helicopter blades to descend smoothly to the ground, where you pull up at the right moment to make a soft landing. I got pretty good at it, but then became a little overconfident. On my last landing, I waited too long to rotate and poked the extended pitot tube in the mud. It got bent. Because of the required repair, the maintenance chief told Ed not to let me do any more engine-out auto rotations. Oh well, it was fun while it lasted.

(The pitot tube is needed to calculate airspeed. By extending it out in front of the aircraft bow wave, you'll get a more accurate true airspeed reading.)

Jerry Werner

USNTPS Helicopter with an

extended pitot tube (orange)

The Murder Board

Most of our flying, as part of the school's curriculum, was testing old aircraft, as if they were new. We had to evaluate the aircraft's ability to do all the aspects of its mission. We documented its strengths and weaknesses. We made recommendations as to whether or not we would accept the airplane, as is, or whether anything needed to be modified.

The importance of the job of a test pilot cannot be overstated. Military aircraft are extremely expensive and the Navy procurement people need to stay within budget. The contractors, who are manufacturing the airplane or its modifications, would be happy to make modifications, as long as the Navy would pay for it. If the changes have to come from their own pocket, they're very resistant.

The test pilot is in a really tough spot when they have to report that the aircraft does not meet a mission requirement or pre-established specification. Some specifications, like top air speed, are easy to measure. But something like handling characteristics during landing or dogfighting is more subjective. The test pilot's assessment that an aircraft does not meet requirements can lead to some heated arguments. There's a lot of pressure on the test pilot to just say OK.

The test pilot school instructors, many of whom were battle tested, helped prepare new test pilots for this experience through what they called a "murder board." Two or three instructors would gang up on the student, role-playing Navy procurement and the contractor, and completely rip apart the report and recommendations. It was intended to be a surprise, so you never knew which of your aircraft evaluation reports would get such treatment. When it was my turn, I should've been better prepared. They found two numbers that did not add up correctly and told me that I lost all credibility and the rest of the report should be tossed out! I got very defensive and angry. I was so tense that I strained some muscles in my back, when I went on my daily workout run. It was an important lesson for me. Chill out. Nothing personal. They're just doing their job.

Joy

On Friday night, January 18, 1980, I experienced *JOY* for the first time in my life. Our first child was born, Matthew Thomas Werner, at the Navy hospital, NAS Patuxent River. He was more than two weeks late and Christine experienced 18 hours of dry labor (premature escape of the amniotic fluid.) It was very difficult and painful for her. The birth was not expensive, $25 out-of-pocket. But sometimes you get what you pay for. Doctors at that tiny naval hospital had little experience delivering babies, so they had to call in a specialist. They waited way too long to bring in somebody who knew what he was doing.

With a new baby at home, it was time to revisit Open Marriage. We had agreed to be flexible about the traditional roles of husband and wife. Christine expected me to help with feeding and diapers in the middle of the night. I had no role models. No male relatives or friends had helped with feeding a baby or changing a diaper. I was willing to do that, but not in the middle of the night. Christine had no job other than to raise the baby and deal with the issues of the home while I was in school. I studied every night till midnight and had to be up at 5:45 AM to be ready for the carpool to school. So when she insisted that I do the 3 o'clock feeding and diaper change, I resented it.

To keep the peace in the family, I took my turn, getting up with the baby in the middle of the night. Then, to get going in the morning on so little sleep, I needed a stimulant. At the age of 32, I finally tried coffee. It worked! But I did not ask anyone else to make it or pay for it.

A journalist's article got my attention, the headline read, "I Am in Love with Three People." She was referring to her husband, son and daughter. I had begun to feel the same way. I was bonding with my son and falling in love. That was the big payoff for helping raise a baby.

Jerry Werner

Baby Matthew and Daddy

"A Number One, Top of the Heap?"

Commander Stu Fitrell sold me on the idea of having our home built in the same neighborhood so we could carpool. That meant that he and I would spend an hour and a half a day, Monday through Friday, for a year, discussing a wide variety of topics. A man with a master's degree in aeronautical engineering, a test pilot school graduate, and a former test pilot, he was qualified to answer any aviation technical questions I could think of. I asked many such questions and learned a lot from him. We also got to know each other very well on other levels.

Stu Fitrell was a character. He was both entertaining and frustrating. He loved to debate any topic. If I took a position, he would take the counter position, and make up "alternate" facts if he had to. Name a subject, any subject: Aircraft carriers, flight simulators, chewing gum, lawnmowers, automobiles, bumper stickers, dependency on foreign oil, car fuel efficiency, religion, distance running, UFOs, ghosts, clairvoyance, vegetarianism, road signs, rearing children (especially teenagers), cheating at the soapbox derby, remotely piloted vehicles…

Captain Stuart Fitrell, 2001

January, 1980, six months before graduation from the test pilot school, Stu said that he would like me to come work for him after graduation, in his Ordnance department. The Navy's newest fighter, the F-18 Hornet, was in development and had not been flown by a Navy test pilot, yet. It was expected to eventually replace the F-4 Phantom, F-14 Tomcat, and the A-7 Corsair.

"Would you like to be the first test pilot to fly the F-18 Hornet?" Stu asked.

I was stunned! Flying and testing the Navy's newest fighter would put me on top of the world!

I responded enthusiastically, "**YES**!"

I did not ask what my testing mission would be, that would come tomorrow. For the rest of the day, I had an otherworldly glow. Everything that I had been working for, all these years, was coming to fruition. If I did a good job of testing the newest fighter, I would certainly be in a competitive position to get into NASA. Mars was in sight.

The McDonnell Douglas F-18 Hornet

I went home and celebrated with Chris, baby Matthew, Pooch and the cats (Muse and Pumpkin)! We toasted with rum 'n Coke…

(Actually, Matthew had milk and Pooch and the kitties had water.)

The next day arrived, the carpool headed south to Pax River, and I asked Stu the inevitable question,

"What capabilities will I be testing on the F-18 Hornet?"

"You will be testing its ability to drop 'shaped' weapons," he responded.

Oh shit!

(Shaped weapons is a euphemism for Weapons of Mass Destruction; nuclear, biological, and chemical weapons, also referred to as NBC)

My heart sank. That was not what I wanted to hear. If I were testing the aircraft's ability to land aboard an aircraft carrier, conduct dog fighting, or even dropping conventional bombs, I would not have given it a second thought. But to perfect its ability to deliver Weapons of Mass Destruction was not even in my Belief system.

I was silent for a long time. I told Stu that I would have to think about it.

Deep soul-searching began. I did not have to reach a decision for six months, and I would take all of that time to decide whether or not to accept that assignment.

I saw a bumper sticker that read, "What would Jesus do?" I didn't know the answer to that question but I intended to find out.

Raised as a Roman Catholic, I had very little exposure to the Bible. Generally, the clergy would share sections of it with us and give us their interpretation. I bought a Catholic Bible and read it from cover to cover. I read the New Testament twice. I was searching for guidance. The Old Testament, based on the Jewish Torah, was replete with justifications for war and killing one's enemies. But the New Testament was supposed to be the Christian's guide book. And I found absolutely no hint of approval for killing enemies, much less mass murdering civilians.

Jesus said:

"Turn the other cheek."

"Love your enemies."

"Do good things to those who despise you."

"Do unto others, as you would have them do unto you."

I met with Navy Chaplains, a Catholic priest and a Protestant minister. I also presented the issue to my hometown priest, Father Crowley, when we traveled to Saint Joseph's Church in Elk Mound, for Matthew's baptism.

The Protestant minister gave me a pamphlet that outlined why killing enemies is permitted by God. Father Crowley gave me a copy of Saint Augustine's book on Just War. And the Navy Catholic Chaplain, Rev. Edward T. Hill gave me a copy of the Navy regulations that allow for change in status to Conscientious Objector (Non-Combatant). He said that the Catholic Church allows its members to participate in a Just War and also supports those who believe there's no justification for killing people at all. He told me something else I did not know, that the Catholic Church, in its first 300 years, was pacifist. They did not believe in taking another person's life for any reason. It wasn't until the Romans made Catholicism their official religion that all the religious "Christian" killing began.

Principles of Just War Theory

Let's take a look at Just War theory, and how it fit into my thinking.

1. Last Resort

A just war can only be waged after all peaceful options are considered. The use of force can only be used as a last resort.

2. Legitimate Authority

A just war is waged by a legitimate authority. A war cannot be waged by individuals or groups that do not constitute the legitimate government.

3. Just Cause

A just war needs to be in response to a wrong suffered. Self-defense against an attack always constitutes a just war; however, the war needs to be fought with the objective to correct the inflicted wound.

4. Probability of Success

In order for a war to be just, there must be a rational possibility of success. A nation cannot enter into a war with a hopeless cause.

5. Right Intention

The primary objective of a just war is to re-establish peace. In particular, the peace after the war should exceed the peace that would have succeeded without the use of force. The use of force must be for justice.

6. Proportionality

The violence in a just war must be proportional to the casualties suffered. The nations involved in the war must avoid disproportionate military action and only use the amount of force absolutely necessary.

7. Civilian Casualties

The use of force must distinguish between the militia and civilians. Innocent citizens must never be the target of war; soldiers should always avoid killing civilians. The deaths of civilians are only justified when they are unavoidable victims of a military attack on a strategic target.

Clearly, if "innocent citizens must never be the target of war," then weapons of mass destruction have no place in a Just War.

MAD

Christine and I attended Catholic Mass, weekly in Virginia Beach, starting the first Sunday after we discovered she was pregnant. When we got to Mechanicsville, we joined the local parish, Our Lady of the Wayside, in Chaptico, Maryland. The presiding priest was Rev Anthony Bonfiglio. I never discussed my moral dilemma with him, until after he delivered a sermon about patriotism in which he said, "Above the flag of every nation stands the cross of Christ." I told him what I was going through, and asked him if that sermon was intended for me. He said it wasn't, but if you believe in signs from God, then it was for me.

I discussed the weapons of mass destruction dilemma with Stu Fitrell on numerous occasions over six months. He had also been raised Catholic. He and his family went to mass on Easter and Christmas. We talked about it from every angle. He said that as a junior officer, he sat on a catapult, ready to launch with a nuclear weapon strapped to his A-4 Skyhawk, during the Cuban Missile Crisis. He decided that if he got airborne that he would drop his bomb, unarmed, in the ocean. They never launched him or anyone else with a nuke. I did not know it at the time, but that was not a true story, it was a parable. He was still in Flight School at the time of the Cuban Missile Crisis.

What I could not understand was why we were asking Navy attack pilots to drop nuclear bombs. We already had the nuclear Triad and Mutual Assured Destruction (MAD). The Triad included hundreds of land-based silos with intercontinental ballistic missiles, thousands of Air Force strategic bombers, and hundreds of submarine-launched warheads on missiles from the U.S. Navy. Between the Soviet Union and the USA, we had enough weapons to destroy the world 10 times over. Why did we need to launch even more nukes from Navy aircraft carriers? It made no sense.

And for a guy like me, who wanted to be an astronaut and explore space, why should I be put in a position where I have to agree to be a mass murderer to do so?

Note to Grandchildren"

When you face a serious moral dilemma or important ethical decision, what will you use as your Guidance? What constitutes your moral compass?

Chapter 11
My Decision and the Fall Out

1980-81

Soul Searching

I want to tell you more about the depth of soul-searching that went on during the six months in which I had to decide whether or not to accept the test pilot assignment. I was scheduled to graduate from the US Naval Test Pilot School, on June 13, 1980. That would complete the accomplishment of my four major Astronaut Track goals, thereby meeting the minimum requirements for entry to NASA. It had taken me 19 years to get there.

As expected, I received the actual orders to report to Stu Fitrell's department, the Naval Test Center Strike Aircraft Directorate, June 16, where I would be expected to fly the new F-18 Hornet and perfect its ability to deliver Weapons of Mass Destruction (WMD). What did that mean? That assignment required that I become intimately familiar with nuclear, biological, and chemical bombs that would be delivered by the Hornet. It meant carrying inert bombs that were the same size, shape, weight, and center of gravity as the real thing. It required the development of procedures and modifications to the aircraft and its systems to make sure that it could effectively and efficiently deliver those "shaped" weapons. In the end, it required writing procedures for pilots to execute such missions.

What did these bombs do when they were dropped? The hydrogen bomb that the Hornet was about to carry was about seven times more powerful than the bombs dropped on Nagasaki and Hiroshima. It was indiscriminate. Exploded over a big city, it would be expected to kill more than a million people. And those killed outright would be the lucky ones.

The biological bomb? I have no idea what biological weapons I would've been working with. The United States signed the Biological Weapons Convention treaty in 1972, which outlawed them. We have some recent experience with Covid-19. If we released a deadly virus, it could kill millions of the enemy, but eventually would come back to bite us, too. Senseless.

And chemical weapons? Chemical weapons, like mustard and nerve gas, are much more limited in scope, but can cause immense suffering to the people affected. They have been banned since World War I for good reason.

The United States was then, and still is, a signatory to the Geneva Conventions of 1925 and 1949 and to the Additional Protocols of 1972 and 1977. Those agreements make the use of WMD against civilians a war crime. War crimes are in the news as

I write this chapter in November 2023. Russia has been accused of war crimes against Ukraine, and the Palestinians and Israelis have accused one another of specifically targeting civilians.

Under what circumstances might a Navy pilot be called upon to deliver WMD?

The United States, then, and now retains the right of first use of nuclear weapons. That means that a flawed human being, called the President of the United States, could order me to deliver WMD against another country and start World War III. While I was considering these possibilities, I was thinking about the previous two presidents. I was concerned the orders could come from someone like Lyndon Johnson, who escalated the war in Vietnam based on a lie about the incident in the Tonkin Gulf. Or they could come from someone like Richard Nixon, who extended the Vietnam War by four years for his own political purposes and then got caught in Watergate.

Did I want to put myself in a position where I was committing a war crime on behalf of someone called "Mr. President?" Could I exonerate myself by using the Nuremberg defense, "I was just following orders."

Are human lives less valuable, just because they're standing on the other side of a line drawn on a map?

What choice should I have made? Accept the assignment or reject the assignment?

What would you do?

I wanted to continue on my astronaut track. After all, I had devoted my whole life to it. Looking for a justification to stay on track, I evaluated the decision on three levels, human, legal, and religious.

On the human level, we would all like to leave the world in better shape for our children and grandchildren. Would my furthering the cause of WMD accomplish that?

On the legal level, both international and US law forbids the use of weapons of mass destruction against civilians.

And finally, the actual change in designation to non-combatant argument, would have to take place on the religious level, where there was no evidence that Jesus would be OK with it.

In an act of self-defense, I had no issue. The fighter pilot role was uncontroversial for me. I was protecting my buddies, my ship, my family, and my country. Shooting down an enemy airplane was all part of the job. There was moral equivalency. We fighter pilots knew we were both intent on defeating each other. If I shot him down, I hoped that he bailed out safely, but I was happy the threat was eliminated.

Based on all of my deliberations, I decided to apply for a change in designation from Combatant to Non-Combatant, as permitted under the Freedom of Religion section of the US Bill of Rights, and spelled out in Navy procedures. The administrative board members were certain to question me about why it took 14 years in the Navy for me to come to that conclusion. I was prepared to answer that question.

The Decision

I was scheduled to meet my new boss at 0900 hr Monday morning, June 16.

My wife Chris and I had been discussing, praying and meditating on the pros and cons of this decision for six months. She had gone through it step-by-step with me and thoroughly understood the implications. She said she would support me regardless of what I decided to do. On Sunday night, I lined up Matthew, Pooch and the two cats, Muse, and Pumpkin. I gave each a hug and a kiss. I knew they would love me, regardless, even if I ended up in jail. (I don't think the cats knew what was going on...)

On Monday morning, I kissed Chris goodbye and drove down to Pax River by myself, parked the car and walked to the meeting room in the Strike Aircraft Test Directorate. My new boss was a Lieutenant Commander like me, but older. (I had recently been promoted.) He reported to Commander Stu Fitrell.

He walked into the room, gave me a firm handshake and began his welcome aboard speech, when I politely interrupted and told him that I had bad news. I said that Stu Fitrell had described the new job to me months ago and I decided to turn down the assignment for moral reasons. I had been in consultation with the Catholic Chaplain and had decided to file for designation as a non-combatant. I said that I was sorry for the problems that my decision would create for him.

He was speechless and had a look on his face that said, WTF! He excused himself and presumably went to consult with the boss. He returned and told me to go home and await instructions.

60 Minutes Episode?

I drove home and awaited instructions. Before the end of the day, I received a phone call from a man who identified himself as Admiral Wissler's Chief of Staff. (Admiral JG Wissler was the senior officer, Commander Naval Air Test Center.) He told me that I was under house arrest until further notice. I was directed to stay in my home and not go anywhere until authorized.

Well, I wasn't in jail, but I was a prisoner in my own home. A week went by and I heard from no one. Another week went by, silence. A third week went by, crickets. The fourth week went by, not a peep.

What was going on? I found out months later that my request for re-designation to non-combatant was unique, in peacetime. No Navy pilot had ever requested such a change in status, except during a war. They did not know what to do with me. I don't know how far up the chain of command the buck was passed, but it took them a long time to decide what to do.

In the meantime, I did chores around the house, cut the grass, and walked around the block with my wife and baby. When it came to shopping, Chris took the car into town and I stayed home and babysat. It also gave me time to polish up my 14 page request for change in status from combatant to non-combatant. I mailed it on July 5th. But I did seriously wonder what was going on and what their plans were for me.

From their point of view, Gerald C. Werner had a spotless record in the Navy for 14 years and had risen to, arguably, top fighter pilot. For him to turn down the best assignment in the world, something had to be wrong with him. He must have gone insane.

What had changed? What was different? I never had to deal with WMD before. I had dropped practice bombs in training, but the simulated targets were all military. I had never been given a mission to intentionally kill civilians, much less murder of them in large numbers. The whole purpose of WMD is to cause as much pain and suffering as possible to a large innocent population.

They wanted to prove me insane for not wanting to kill a million people and their pets. That would be difficult.

Finally, in my fifth week of house arrest, I received a phone call from the Admiral's secretary, who said that I was to report to the Chief Flight Surgeon at the US Naval Hospital in Bethesda, Maryland, at 0900 Wednesday, July 23. For what? For a psychiatric evaluation, of course.

The Chief Flight Surgeon was Captain William W. Simmons, USN. I spent the whole day there, and he was a real gentleman from beginning to end. His assistants administered a variety of psychological tests and evaluations over a six hour period. In the final meeting of the day, he told me that he was going to recommend my designation as a conscientious objector and removal from combat flying, as requested. He found no mental or emotional illness. He gave me the impression that he respected the stand that I was taking and that, under similar circumstances, he might have done the same.

Then he did something unexpected. He handed me a piece of paper with his home phone number. I did not know why.

I went back home. Another week passed before hearing from anyone. Then I got a call from the Admiral's secretary. I was being sent back to Bethesda for a second opinion. What? They were not able to prove me crazy during six hours of interrogation, so they wanted another crack at it.

That evening, I called Captain Simmons' home phone number. His wife picked up. I explained who I was and why I was calling. I wanted to know if Captain Simmons could tell me why I was being called back for a second evaluation. She said her husband was not home. The Navy had shipped him off to Guam, on short notice, and she did not know why. She sounded scared. She gave me the impression that she was worried that her phone might be tapped. I thanked her for her time and told her that I hoped her husband was not in trouble because of me. I asked her to thank him for me. Was I in the middle of a 60 Minutes episode?

On August 5, I returned to Bethesda Naval Hospital and was introduced to the doctor who would be leading the testing for the day, Lieutenant JH Kleiger, Ph.D. He was a bad cop to Captain Simmons, good cop. He had an aggressive, in your face, attitude towards me from beginning to end. He seemed hell bent on proving that I was crazy.

Dr. Kleiger and his staff administered the MMPI, Rorschach Technique, Thematic Apperception Test, Conceptual Level Angology Test, Object Sorting Test, subsets of the Wechsler Adult Intelligence Scale, and Projective Sentence Completion Test. A couple of these were repeats from my first visit. I remember most vividly Dr. Kleiger, himself, administered the Rorschach (ink blot) test. He showed me what could be perceived as a blood-spattered room. I told him that it looked like my baby boy got carried away with splashing his grape juice and strawberry jam. He gave me a look that said, "You gotta be shitting me." With all of the bloody Rorschach inkblots, I chose a more benign interpretation of each. He did not like that.

I came into the testing with some knowledge of psychology. I read a few books in high school, I subscribed to Psychology Today for a few years, and I took a course at the Naval Academy. I had a pretty good idea of what they were looking for in each test.

I left that day without knowing how I fared on the tests, but I could not believe that they proved anything negative. The final report was not completed until August 22. I did not see it until my administrative hearings, months later.

Dr. Kleger's conclusion was interesting: "In sum, the results of the testing are not consistent with an underlying thought disorder. It is, however, striking that the patient's extremely defensive test taking style should differ so markedly from his clinical presentation. Such a discrepancy may reflect the patient's skill in manipulating and misleading others."

My opinion: Any guy, in my shoes, who was not extremely defensive, probably had something wrong with him!

It appeared as if the doctor was saying:

"Support for WMD = Sane.

Questioning WMD = Not Sane."

I received a call from the Admiral's secretary the week of August 25. She said I was to report to the Admiral the next day in his office at the Naval Air Station, Patuxent River.

I made the 45 minute drive. I was nervous. I did not know how people were going to look at me or treat me. I first met with his secretary. It was a chilly reception. She took me to Admiral Wissler's office. It was a big space, but otherwise unpretentious. He acted like he was annoyed that he had to deal with me. He was definitely not friendly. But I didn't expect him to be. He said that I had passed the psychological tests at Bethesda and he would choose the administrative board members who would hear my case.

A Job for a Non-Combatant

Surprisingly, he already had a non-combat job for me. One of his projects had gone awry, was way behind schedule and needed a project manager to get it back on track. It was a very unusual project. The Test Center was converting a retired commercial airliner to an aerial refueling tanker. Why were they doing that?

Because they would be doing extensive testing of the F-18 Hornet, an aircraft already known to be fuel limited. They needed a tanker to arrive at the same time the Hornet did. Given an airborne tanker, the Hornet could remain in the air for hours of testing. Why not use a regular Navy tanker? The fleet did not have any extras. Why not buy a new one? It wasn't in the budget and would've taken too long to build.

The next day, I was introduced to the current project manager. He was a Navy Commander, much senior to me, but was not full-time on the project. He had other responsibilities and that could make a big difference. I would be on it full-time. He shared his project plan and budget documentation.

Over the next few days, I was introduced to the team members. I had one full-time employee, a 65-year-old man, twice retired, who was deaf in one ear and couldn't hear out of the other. (A joke of his) He was a retired Navy Gunner who probably needed better hearing protection when he was a young enlisted man. His second retirement came from civil service. He turned out to be a very valuable team member, as he knew Test Center people, places, and procedures, which I did not. I could ask him any question and he either had the answer or could find it quickly. He was my Google of 1980!

The remaining dozen team members were all specialists, aircraft, budget, construction, legal, operations, procurement, and a couple of PhD scientists.

The Convair 880 Flown by Trans World Airlines (TWA)

What was the status of the project the day I took over? They had already identified the aircraft they wanted to use: a retired commercial airliner, 4-jet engine Convair 880 that had been flown by Trans World Airlines (TWA). They had taken it from the desert, where it was in "mothballs" and were preparing it to fly again. They had also identified an aerial refueling package, taken from a retired Navy tanker, that would fit it in the rear of the Convair 880.

In the 1960s, when the F-4 Phantom was setting all kinds of speed records for fighters, the Convair 880 was setting speed records for commercial airliners. Not surprisingly it had the same engines as the Phantom, J-79s, but without afterburners. This aerial refueling project will run in parallel with the other stories that are about to unfold.

Investigation into the Circumstances Surrounding…

The next drama involved the hearings to determine whether or not the Navy would change my designation to non-combatant. The Investigating Officer, CDR Maurice Manahan, met with me on October 3. He scheduled the first meeting with the panel on October 29. Based on his initial interview questions, he gave me the impression that he thought I had some ulterior motive. Eventually, I learned that he and many others thought that I was trying to get out of my four years of obligated Test Pilot School payback by getting a defense contractor job for big bucks. That, of course, was not true.

As a result of my sense of their distrust, the hearing's title had a rather sinister ring to it:

"Investigation into the circumstances surrounding the application for classification as Conscientious Objector, Class 1-A-0 (non-combatant) by LCDR Gerald C Werner, USN"

Was I still in a 60 Minutes episode?

All branches of the military service have procedures to follow when someone requests to be designated as a Conscientious Objector 1-O (non-participant) or 1-A-O (non-combatant.) I was requesting designation as a non-combatant, so I could complete my remaining four years of service to my country.

The Navy document that described how to deal with this situation was the Bureau of Naval Personnel (BUPERS) Manual Section 1860110. It outlined all the requirements, those of the applicant and those of the investigators. Here are some of the questions I was required to answer - under oath - before the panel:

- Religion: Parents and spouse

- Thorough description of the nature of the belief which requires the applicant to seek assignment to non-combatant status

- How the applicant's beliefs have changed or developed

- Explanation of when and why these beliefs became incompatible with military service

- An explanation of the circumstances, if any, under which the applicant believes in the use of force

- How the applicant's daily lifestyle has changed as a result of his beliefs

- Explanation in the applicant's opinion of what most conspicuously demonstrates the consistency and depth of his beliefs

- Applicant's religious organization

- How the applicant became a member of the organization

- Name and location of church he attends

- Name and title of the present pastor at the church

- Supporting certification signed by an authorized personal religious counselor (such as his/her minister) who would attest that:

  - Applicant is presently an active member of the religious group and in good standing

  - Applicant regularly attends services consistent with the religious practice

  - Religious counselor believes the member is sincere in his commitment to this religious faith

  - Recommendation from a Navy Chaplain

The hearings began with my being under fire for having taken the stand that I did. They could not understand how someone as successful as I was could possibly throw it all away. They were quite accusatory, at times, sarcastic. But over the four weeks, the jury learned that I was sincere and did not have any ulterior motives. When the hearings ended, after Thanksgiving, some were apologetic for having attacked me the way they had.

I kept all of my arguments and justification within the religious bounds. I did not ask why Navy airplanes were carrying WMD. The answer to that question was well above everybody's paygrade. I did not get into war crimes, either. That could cause all kinds of distractions. I stuck to the script: Christianity, Just War theory, and every parent's desire for a peaceful world for his children and grandchildren.

My character witnesses,

1. Father Thomas Crowley, Pastor of Saint Joseph's Church in Elk Mound, Wisconsin. Introduced in the first chapter, was an important mentor who helped me get a nomination to a service academy and followed my career for 14 years. He was an enlisted man in the US Navy during World War II. He believed that WWII was a Just War.

2. CDR Stuart Fitrell, Head of the Strike Aircraft Test Directorate, my carpool buddy for a year, recruited me to come work for him and let me know six months in advance that it would involve WMD. We had many hours of discussion about it.

3. Lieutenant Greg "Tokyo" Rose, test pilot school classmate. Tokyo and I had been "enemies" when I was in VF-102 and he was in VF-33 on the USS Independence. We were keen competitors at Top Gun. But we became close friends after

we arrived at test pilot school together. I shared with him what I was going through months before the hearings.

All three gentlemen provided strong endorsements. They confirmed that they believed that I was sincere in my convictions and should be granted the change in designation. But they said they would not have made the same decision, if they were in my shoes.

While I very much appreciated their testimony, my best character witness turned out to be the Catholic Chaplain, CDR Edward T. Hill. In a way, he also became my legal counsel. The Navy did not provide me with an attorney. So Father Hill, with assistance from the American Civil Liberties Union (ACLU), served as my counsel. I share with you, on the next three pages, his complete written testimony. It is also a good summary of topics that were covered in the actual hearings and arguments made in favor of re-designation to non-combatant. Reading this decades later, I am still moved by the power of his testimony.

Navy Chaplain's Testimony

From: Commander Edward T. Hill, CHC, USN, (SSN), Catholic Chaplain, Naval Air Station, Patuxent, River, MD 20670

To: To Whom It May Concern

Subject: LCDR G. C. Werner, Conscientious Objector; application for.

1. Gerald Chester Werner (32) has been counseled by me for several months. He is married, his wife's name is Christine; they have a son, Matthew, who is eight months old.

2. Lieutenant Commander Werner's catharsis is admirably described in his own statement. Through counseling, I can attest to his sincerity, honesty, and integral personality. His confidence is already demonstrated by a successful career, spanning 32 years.

3. Lieutenant Commander Werner has integrity, a manliness that marks him above the average hero; he is willing to suffer the consequences of his convictions; he puts his life behind his words, and hides nothing from the ridicule and wrath of legitimate authority. He has been the sternest jury and strictest judge in his own case. He is not proud of his

behavior in the past; in fact, he recounts the scars as though witnessing at an AA meeting.

4. The value of life has become a repeating paean to Gerald Werner. The seed could have been sown by a radical, Reverend Daniel Barragan, S.J., but he attributes his enlightenment to John Paul II. Actually, the bishops of the Catholic Church in the United States of America, with Cardinal Krol of Philadelphia, as their spokesman, testified before the Senate Foreign Relations Committee:

   a. "… The fact is that we cannot avoid speaking the truth about war in our day. God created us in his image and likeness; he gave us life, and endowed us with inalienable rights to life and liberty. War involves the taking of life, and nuclear war threatens human life on this planet in a qualitatively new way. No more war. War, never again. (America, 3-8-80)

5. Bupers Notice 1900 (8 October 1971) denotes the Chaplain as a religious expert. In that light, it is essential to point out that Christians of the first three centuries believed that the example of Jesus and the teaching of the gospel counseled them to renounce participation in war. With the establishment of Christianity as the official religion of the empire in the fourth century, more and more Christians

identified their own welfare, and protection of the church, with the strength and integrity of the Roman state. This development led to norms of deciding when a person could justly participate in war. From that time, they existed within the Christian community, both those who admitted the possibility of a Just War and those who adhered to the teachings of non-violence. This dilemma endures to the present day,

6. February 14, 1980. The Administrative Board of the US Catholic Conference reflected that dilemmas dimensions when it said:

    a. "We acknowledge the right of the state to register citizens, for the purpose of military conscription, both in peacetime, and in times of national emergency… While acknowledging the duty of the state to defend society, and its correlative right to use force in certain circumstances, we also affirm the Catholic teachings of the state's decision to use force should always be morally scrutinized by citizens asked to support the decision or participate in war… We regard this question and all its dimensions as a central element in Catholic teaching on the morality of war. First, we support the right of conscientious objection as a valid, moral position, derived from the

> gospel and Catholic teaching… Second, we support the right of selective conscientious objection (SCO) as a moral conclusion which can be validly derived from the classical moral teaching of Just-War theory."

7. The United States government also recognizes the status of conscientious objection for <u>religious</u>, moral, and ethical reasons by providing for it in the law. The US government, however, does not recognize selective conscientious objection.

8. Lieutenant Commander Werner claims the right to conscientious objection on the basis of religious principle, derived from the gospel and Catholic teaching. He is sincere in his convictions; it is a valid, moral position.

9. Lieutenant Commander Werner does not stand like the jolly green giant, akimbo to the United States of America. Rather with the reverence of George Washington, he kneels and prays President Eisenhower's words (Congressional Act 14, June 1954) for adding "Under God" to the Pledge of Allegiance: … In this way, we are reaffirming the transcendence of religious faith in America's heritage and future; in this way we shall constantly strengthen the

spiritual weapons, which forever will be our country's most powerful resource in peace and war.

10. It is apparent through counseling that Lieutenant Commander Werner is accepting more responsibility for the welfare of the USA – a quiet Patrick Henry, witnessing for higher values, focusing on the stars in the flag.

11. As the challenging religious officer expert, it was necessary to keep in mind that the least complicated claim of Christianity is its greatest truth: love is the strongest force in the universe. Only the man who is willing to go on his knees, ever understood that truth. Gerald Werner has a firm grasp of this truth and has become a giving person, he willingly sacrifices himself for others; he respects the value of life and the dignity of human mankind. He does not criticize or condemn anyone. His actions are motivated by his faith. He may seem out of step with the modern world, but there is nothing sissy about this man who walks with God.

12. After 14 years in the Navy, a graduate of the US Naval Academy, and the US Naval Test Pilot School, Gerald Werner is by US military admission, <u>a cut above</u>. Now he has been subjected to scrutiny, psychological search, mental harassment, overt discrimination and petty prejudices….

13. If he stands the torture well, he will be acknowledged as strong, the system could not break him. If he caves in quickly, he'll be seen as weak, and this, too, will damage the name of the system that elevated him in light of his leadership qualities. A simple solution would be to shoot him; and Gerald Werner would accept that sentence with the silence of Christ. But the Navy does not want to shoot him. The Navy wants Gerald Werner to work for them again. He is honorbound, to fulfill his commitment and serve out his military obligation. He has no hesitation in doing this. An embarrassment surfaces, when individuals with authority vent their ire and try to punish him for his religious conviction.

14. <u>The solution</u>: The Military Selective Service Act (Public Law, 129, 92nd Congress) (Approved, September 28, 1971) directs that Gerald Werner, a conscientious objector in the Navy, be assigned to noncombatant service. He will fulfill his contract with the Navy for four years of duty; he will continue to serve well.

15. I have questioned Gerald Werner actively, extensively, critically, and for weeks; I am convinced he is conscientiously opposed to participation in the violence we call warfare. He maintains his position on solid religious

principles, advocated by the Catholic Church and supported by his family. I tested his beliefs in various trials: tennis competition, light conversation, contrived situations, routine observation, family forays, and regular counseling. He's not solipsistic, but genuinely committed to these lofty goals of religious non-violence and universal peace. He is open and responsive, with a humility that is totally disarming.

Signed

Edward T Hill.

Chaplain Hill's testimony was cogent, comprehensive, and powerful. But would it be enough?

Chapter 12

The Conclusion

Findings, Opinions, and Recommendations

In December 1980, I was waiting on the decision and final report from the investigating committee.

There is irony in the withering criticism that was aimed at me. I was surrounded by Naval Academy graduates. While in college, we were all required to go to church every Sunday. A Christian prayer was recited before every meal, thanking God. What were we supposed to learn from our Christian immersion? The Prince of Peace was not our guide, after all?

In addition to religion, at USNA, we also got lectures about military law. It was clear, based on our studies of the Geneva Conventions, that attacking civilian populations was a war crime. An order from a senior officer to commit a war crime was an illegal order. Weren't we expected to uphold the Constitution by refusing to carry out an illegal order? Now, they could argue that I was not being asked to kill anyone at the Test Center. Yes, but from my point of view, to spend two years perfecting a system's ability to kill a maximum number of people, efficiently, is way worse than being asked to drop a single bomb. These systems and procedures would have my fingerprints all over them.

On December 5, CDR Manahan submitted the investigative committee's report to the Admiral. They found me sincere in my beliefs and recommended that the Navy change my designation to non-combatant and allow me to complete my 3.5 years of remaining service.

Admiral JG Wissler concurred with their recommendation and passed it on to his superiors, on December 17. He said:

- Lieutenant Commander Werner meets the criteria for conscientious objector, class 1-A-O, as supported by the investigation, by his unquestioned sincerity, and by his recent and current lifestyle.

- Lieutenant Commander Werner's professional performance, and personal conduct continue to be superb. Following application for conscientious objector status, he was reassigned to my staff as project officer for modifications to a Convair 880 civil transport aircraft to an aerial tanker configuration. He has not been in an active flying status since that time.

- In my opinion, Lieutenant Commander Werner would be a valuable asset to the Navy performance wise, including non-combatant flying, if an appropriate billet/organizational situation exists elsewhere. Continued assignment to the

Naval Air Test Center is unacceptable and inconsistent with requirements of this command's mission, professional military staffing, and morale.

So, the Admiral agreed that I should be able to complete my remaining 3.5 years in the Navy, as a non-combatant, just not on his base. At first, I was angry about this. Then, given time for it to sink in, I realized it was a compliment. He found me so credible, that he was worried that I might convince someone else to follow in my footsteps. That could be a disaster for his career. And in the end, the risk to everybody's career was the overriding concern. "What are my superiors going to think if I am found agreeing with this guy?"

The Admiral's recommendation was submitted to the head of the Naval Military Personnel Command in December, 1980. I had no idea how long it would take them to decide what to do with me. No matter, I had an important project to get done - on time and within budget - the Convair 880 program.

The Convair 880 Program

The primary mission of the Convair 880 would be to refuel the F-18 Hornet and other aircraft. So the first order of business for me was to make absolutely sure there existed a large area of smooth air behind the airliner, within a range of reasonable air speeds, so another aircraft could refuel from that position.

My contractors were working on the aircraft at NAS Mojave, in the California Mojave Desert, about 100 miles northeast of Los Angeles. I visited them monthly.

On my first visit, I took off from the naval air station in a T-33, and rendezvoused with the Convair 880, both shown below before taxi. I checked out the smoothness of the air in the range of distance the fuel hose would feed a receiving aircraft. Fortunately, the space behind and below the Convair was a really big range of tranquility. I knew we were on the right track.

T-33 T-Bird and Convair 880, NAS Mojave

My responsibilities as the project manager were:

- Managing the contractors

- Observing the refurbishment and installation of the aerial refueling hose package at NAS Mohave

- Building a facility for the pilots, maintenance personnel and spare parts storage at Pax River

- Ordering and receiving spare parts

- Hiring the pilots

- Testing the operational readiness of the Convair 880 tanker

- Marketing additional uses of the 880 aircraft with the East Coast Navy

The Military Industrial Complex

I was invited to present the Convair 880 program at the Annual Aerial Refueling Conference. This event is a forum for the international air mobility and airlift community to discuss the latest developments in aerial refueling technology and operations, training, and the future of aerial refueling. The conference is typically attended by representatives from government, industry, military and academia. My audience included members from the US Congress, Air Force generals, and defense contractors.

To demonstrate how politically naïve I was, I actually believed the house was packed, standing room only, because they loved my program. It was an opportunity to reuse existing resources and save taxpayers a ton of money. But that was not what the military-industrial complex wanted. They were a polite audience, but once I finished my presentation, they surrounded me like vultures. They made it clear that they would use their political influence to kill the program. There would be no more conversions. (The Convair 880 project, including pilots, spare parts, and offices, cost less than $1 million. The newest tanker, at the time, was the KC-10. It came in at around $35 million per copy.)

Time proved in their favor. They successfully killed the program. The plan for converting three more tankers was scrapped. There would be only one.

The Pentagon

Here's another politically naïve procurement story. My own project, by June, was essentially complete, on time and below budget by around $40,000. My contractor suggested that he spend the remaining budget on a nice carpet in the aircraft. I said NO. I wanted to come in under budget and I saw no reason for a fancy carpet in a military airplane. But he ignored my denial and went over my head to Procurement at the Pentagon, with whom he had the contract, and got approval. He then installed a $40,000 red carpet. I was furious. I drove my car from Pax River to Washington, DC and went to the Pentagon to talk directly with my procurement guy. I told him I wanted the money back in my account. He told me that, obviously, I did not know how things worked at the Pentagon. When it comes to budget money, "Use it or lose it." He allowed the expense and did not back me up.

Mission Accomplished

With the support facilities and people in place, the Convair 880 was delivered to Pax River from the Mojave Desert in mid March, 1981. I performed a couple of takeoffs and landings, with coaching from my contractor pilots, Compton and Longley. I was amazed at how difficult it was to fly a large airplane with mechanical controls. I was accustomed to nimble, quickly responsive airplanes, like the A-4 Skyhawk and the T-38 Talon. In comparison, this big hunk of aluminum and steel, full of fuel, was very slow to respond to any control inputs. It required anticipation and patience when changing speed, direction and rate of descent during approach to landing. It gave me a better appreciation for the challenges commercial pilots face when landing large aircraft, full of passengers and cargo, especially in bad weather.

We completed the testing and the Convair 880 proved successful in its mission to refuel the F-18 Hornet. The Hornet could then stay airborne for hours of flight testing, rather than land to top off every hour and a half.

Convair 880, F-18 Hornet Refueling

New Career?

While I was waiting six months for the Navy to finally decide what to offer me, I began to prepare for a new career, as a civilian. How could I put my training and education to good use and make the world a better place? I was very concerned about our dependence on foreign oil. It appeared to be a continuing root cause of war. If I could find a way to reduce our use of oil, I could make an individual contribution. If I were able to get in a leadership position, I could leverage the multiplier effect.

Reducing our use of oil also had positive effects on cleaner air and reduced carbon in the atmosphere. We were only beginning to take notice of shrinking glaciers and rising sea levels. The 1970s set heat records. There was a lot of public argument over whether or not global warming was a short term aberration, or a long-term trend. There was no general public agreement that human beings were contributing to the majority of the temperature change.

I went to the library and did some research. I learned about opportunities in energy conservation, solar and wind. I read books about all three. The most exciting was wind power, because I could leverage my aero-mechanical education and skills.

Non-Combat Flying Job Found

In the spring of 1981, I had been waiting for months to hear from the Navy as to whether or not they had a new home for me. Then I received a call from my detailer in Washington, DC. First, he told me how impressed he was with what I had done. He revealed that I was the only pilot in the history of the Navy to have requested re-designation to non-combatant status in peacetime. He was effusive. (I was very surprised. Nearly all strangers were judgmental about the decision I made.) He said he had never met anyone with such an impressive record and he had good news, he found a commanding officer who agreed. The CO was interested in having me come to his squadron. I would be flying a non-combat aircraft, the EA-6B Prowler, at NAS Whidbey Island, Puget Sound, Washington State. I would qualify for the current aviator extension bonus of $30,000 ($100,000 2023 dollars). (The bonus was in place to entice naval aviators from my group to extend their service, because of the big pilot shortage.)

EA-6B Prowler

The EA-6B Prowler mission provided electronic warfare (EW) support to Navy and Marine Corps strike aircraft. The Prowler was equipped with a variety of electronic warfare systems that could jam enemy radar, communications, and electronic countermeasures (ECMs). This allowed strike aircraft to operate in heavily defended airspace without being detected or intercepted by enemy air defenses. This mission did not call for the use of bombs, rockets, or missiles.

The Final Navy Decision, to Stay or to Leave

June 7, 1981, six months after I was found both sane and sincere, the Navy finally made its determination and its lawyers offered me two paths. I would not be staying at Patuxent River.

<u>Option 1</u>: Leave the Navy with an Honorable Discharge. Receive no bonus.

(Choose a new career, live at home with family and help raise the children.)

<u>Option 2</u>: Transfer to NAS Whidbey Island, complete three years as a pilot and department head. Pilot the EA-6B Prowler, a non-combat aircraft. Extend an additional two years, if desired, receive a $30,000 bonus ($100,000 in 2023 dollars).

(Expect three to five straight years of sea duty, away from home on board ships about 80% of the time, with very little involvement with raising the children. Distance from Christine's mother, ~3000 miles.)

Which option would you choose?

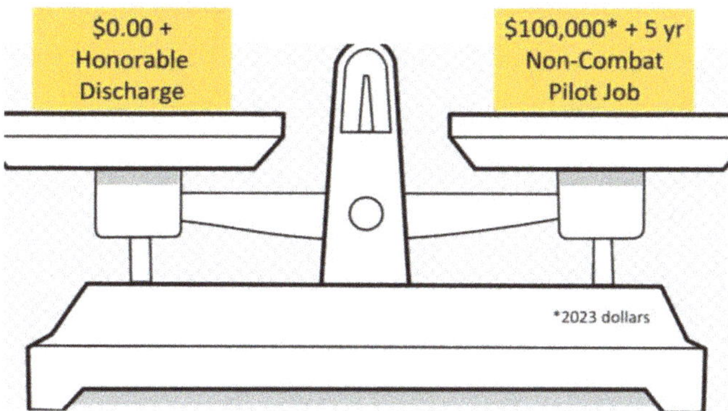

Which one did we choose?

I had promised Christine that if I were no longer on track to be an astronaut, I would get out of the Navy and help raise the babies. That was my word, my commitment. I chose Option 1.

On June 30, 1981, we shipped our household goods and packed up Matthew, Pooch, Muse and Pumpkin and headed to Connecticut. We started an exciting new chapter in our lives. On a wing and a prayer, we began the search for that big house in the country, a new, more peaceful profession and more children together.

Grateful to Be an American

Most countries around the world advertise religious freedom, but few follow through. About a third of the world's countries claim to respect conscientious objection, but most do not guarantee it. I'm grateful to be an American citizen for our Constitution and Bill of Rights. I know all religious views are allowed in our country.

I am also delighted that I was a member of the US Navy. After the brief "60 Minutes" episode, they took my situation seriously and finally offered fair options.

Eleven years after my drama, President H.W. Bush, a World War II Navy pilot and war hero, ordered the removal of weapons of mass destruction from all Navy surface ships. While there were several good reasons for doing so (end of the Cold War, lower risk and cost), I believe his own personal experience as a Navy pilot influenced his decision. Since then, no other Navy pilot has had to face the same dilemma that I did.

And finally, the American Catholic bishops came through, too. In their 1980 document "The Bishops' Statement on Nuclear Weapons," they stated that "the production, possession, and deployment of nuclear weapons are morally wrong." They argued that "nuclear weapons pose an unacceptable threat to human life and the environment, and that their use would be a grave violation of the moral principles of the just war tradition."

In 1983, they added that Catholics involved with nuclear weapons should:

- Work to redirect their skills and labor to more peaceful endeavors. Catholics should seek out employment opportunities that do not contribute to the production or use of nuclear weapons. If they are unable to find other work, they should try to minimize their involvement in the nuclear weapons industry."

Bob Cabana, Astronaut and Friend

Bob "Copa" Cabana was my classmate at the Naval Academy. We were in the same company for four years and played on the same intramural sports teams. His hometown was Minneapolis, so we once shared the driving duties on the way to Annapolis. When I was driving, Bob, who had lookout duty, dozed off and a Wisconsin Trooper pulled me over for speeding. During our dating days, he got to know Chris and I became acquainted with his girlfriend, Nancy. We enjoyed each other's company.

I did not share my long-term astronaut goals with many people, but I did share them with Bob. He did not show any interest in becoming an astronaut while we were at USNA, but was enthused about flying.

After graduation, Bob and Nancy married. He joined the Marine Corps, as an aviator. We found ourselves together in Pensacola flight school. At the same time, Nancy gave birth to a baby boy and I was honored to be asked to be godfather to their first born.

Bob had a successful career with the Marine Corps and was selected for the US Naval Test Pilot School following me, in 1981. He got selected to the astronaut program in 1985, and flew four flights on the space shuttle, two as Mission commander. He invited my family and me to watch his launch in the summer of 1994. I brought my two sons, Matt and Mike. We observed from the designated area. I told you that two F-4 Phantoms taking off, side-by-side at Key West, was obnoxiously loud. But they were mild compared with the Earth shattering volume of the Space Shuttle launch. Awesome!

He was named Chief Astronaut in 1994 and was eventually promoted to Deputy Director of the Johnson Space Center in 2004. In 2008 he was promoted to a really big job, Director of the Kennedy Space Center, responsible for more than 10,000 employees and contractors for the next 12.5 years. In his final job, 2021, he was the top civil servant at NASA and retired at the end of 2023. He is also in the Astronaut Hall of Fame. In my opinion, Robert D. Cabana was a very important influencer in America's space program, especially in transitioning the Space Center from the Shuttle era to the post Shuttle era. Enter SpaceX, Blue Origin, Boeing and Sierra Nevada Corporation.

Bob "Copa" Cabana

I tell you all of this, so that you understand my access to information about the space program and NASA, all of these years. Bob gave me multiple tours, some behind the scenes, and answered all of my questions, except those that might reveal classified information. At times, I lived vicariously through Bob's exciting Space Shuttle experiences.

I did not discuss the WMD issue with him until after I made my decision. He was supportive of my decision, but like all of my friends who were still in uniform, he did not indicate that he agreed with it. We joked that, as a result of my jumping off the astronaut track, Bob got my seat on the Space Shuttle.

Why Aren't We on Mars, Yet?

This book began with my desire to walk on Mars, and my entire astronaut track journey was aimed at that goal. As a 13 year old in 1961, it seemed like that trip should be right around the corner. But here we are today, 54 years since the first man walked on the moon, and we still don't have a flight to Mars scheduled on the calendar. It felt to me that - every decade since the Apollo program - we were close to traveling to Mars. I believe we are no more than 10 years away, in 1980, when I made my decision to turn down the test center assignment.

What happened to our Mars plans since? NASA got stuck in low earth orbit with the Space Shuttle and International Space Station. While those were important steps to space travel, they were not space travel. Here we are in 2024, again we're being told it'll be another 10 years before humans travel to Mars.

The Surface of the Planet Mars

Below, Google's artificial intelligence application, Bard, gives its answer to the question, "Why hasn't the American space program landed a human being on Mars, yet?"

"There are several reasons why the American space program has not yet put a human being on Mars.

Technical challenges:

- **The long journey:** Mars is about 142 million miles from Earth, and it takes about six months to travel between the two planets. This long journey exposes astronauts to the risks of radiation, isolation, and boredom.

- **The harsh Martian environment:** Mars is a cold, dry, and dusty place with a thin atmosphere. This makes it difficult for humans to survive there, and it requires sophisticated technology to protect them from the harsh environment.

- **The high cost of space travel:** Space travel is very expensive, and sending a human mission to Mars would be the most expensive space mission ever undertaken.

Political and economic challenges:

- **Lack of political will:** There is not currently a strong political will in the United States to send humans to Mars.

This is due in part to the high cost of the mission and the lack of a clear economic or strategic benefit.

- **Competing priorities:** There are other priorities for NASA, such as developing new technology for space exploration and studying climate change. These priorities compete with the goal of sending humans to Mars for funding and resources.

Challenges related to the human body:

- **Long-term effects of radiation:** Exposure to radiation in space can have long-term health effects, including cancer and heart disease. Astronauts on a Mars mission would be exposed to significantly more radiation than astronauts on missions to the Moon or the International Space Station.

- **Psychological effects of isolation:** Astronauts on a Mars mission would be isolated from Earth for the 12 month round-trip plus the time spent on Mars itself. This could have significant psychological effects, including depression, anxiety, and post-traumatic stress disorder.

- **Physical effects of microgravity:** The long-term effects of microgravity on the human body are not fully understood. Astronauts on a Mars mission would spend the six month trip in microgravity, which could lead to bone loss, muscle atrophy, and other health problems.

Despite these challenges, there is still a strong desire to send humans to Mars. The American space program has a long history of exploration and achievement, and many people believe that sending humans to Mars is the next logical step in human exploration.

There are several proposals for how to send humans to Mars, and NASA is currently working on plans to send a human mission to Mars in the 2030s. If these plans are successful, we will finally see humans walking on Mars within the next few decades."

Now, at 75 years old, I view Mars as a harsh tourist destination with no air to breathe, no water to drink, and no protection from bombarding radiation. The mission, including the round trip and the time on the surface of Mars, will take about three years. That means going for three years without a shower or a salad. I would miss my wife, children, grandchildren, other family, friends and my dog Remington.

In the meantime, I have enjoyed my life on Earth very much.

Epilogue

Lofty Goals

Let's be clear, if you set your sights on lofty goals, there is no straight line from A to Z. There are advancing steps, back steps, side steps, missed steps, broken steps, two steps forward and three steps back. In spite of what the media might tell you, there's no such thing as an overnight success. It takes time. My personal observation is that it takes about 10 years to accomplish something really significant. Malcolm Gladwell, in his book "Outliers," says it takes 10,000 hours.

Gladwells's rule goes something like this: "It takes 10,000 hours of intensive practice to achieve mastery of complex skills and materials, like playing the violin, or getting as good as Bill Gates at computer programming."

Currently, the financial services firm, Raymond James, has a slogan: "Life well planned." Nonsense! Life never turns out according to plan.

Let's take a look at how many times I had to change plans because I failed to get to the next step on my astronaut track.

Jerry Werner

Failures:

1. No appointment to the Air Force Academy

2. Failed Initial Navy Physical Exam - flat feet

3. Failed Naval Aviation Physical Exam - deviated septum

4. Underwater swim - failed 200 times

5. Primary Flight Training Grades - < Minimum Required for Jets

6. No initial Acceptance to Graduate School - Low undergrad GPA

7. Basic Jet Flight Training - 3 Downs (flight failures)

8. Expelled from Graduate School - GPA fell below 3.00

9. Failed to be selected to continue flying jets

10. Plowed back - Failed to get selected to a fighter squadron

11. Failed to receive Commanding Officer endorsement for fighters

12. Failed to acquire Executive Officer endorsement for fighters

13. Received a "Bad" performance evaluation from VF-102 CO

14. Nearly killed Commanding Officer on a night catapult shot

15. Received an ethically unacceptable assignment, testing WMD

16. Under House Arrest for 10 weeks

Today's media devotes nearly all of its attention to those who are tougher, faster, louder, smarter and prettier than the rest. But the most valuable asset is persistence. Your persistence, in the face of adversity, will determine your success. As I revealed in Chapter 1, the tortoise wins the race.

Conclusion

I have been invited to tell my story, in a public forum, a number of times over the years. When I get to the end and reveal that I chose not to continue towards the space program, I invariably end up with a room full of tears. But, don't cry for me, Argentina! I have lived a very happy and fulfilling life, more so than if I had stayed on the astronaut track.

What would my life have been like if I had stayed in the Navy and participated in NASA's programs? First, I would not have gotten to Mars because no one has. Second, I would not have done any interplanetary space travel because no one has. And third, I would've been stuck in low earth orbit. While the Space Shuttle was an exciting machine, Bob Cabana only got four flights in 11 years. I would've been greatly disappointed. Astronaut Scott Kelly reveals his experience living almost a year on the International Space

Station in his excellent book, "Endurance." But that experience is not appealing to me, either.

There is one other topic we have not touched upon. It's the 600 pound gorilla in the room. Guilt. If I had devoted two years of my life, my time, energy and intellect to perfecting systems of mass murder, I don't know if I could have lived with myself.

How about family separation? Chris and I thought that NASA would be perfect, like permanent Navy shore duty. But as it turns out, NASA astronauts experienced more family separation than Navy sea duty. I would not have been happy with that.

Bob Cabana turned out to be a much better choice for an astronaut than I ever would have been. If somehow, by my being selected, Bob was not, the whole space program would have suffered the loss of a great contributor!

While this book has focused primarily on my professional goals, I have personal goals, just like anyone else: health, wealth, and happiness. I have been blessed in all regards!

Thank you for riding along on this journey with me and my grandchildren. I look forward to meeting and hearing from you. I leave you with the words of the philosopher, Henry David Thoreau:

"If one advances confidently in the direction of his dreams, and endeavors to live the life which he has imagined, he will meet with a success unexpected in common hours."

Favorite Songs of 1980-81

- Bette Davis Eyes by Kim Carnes

- Endless Love by Diana Ross and Lionel Richie

- Jessie's Girl by Rick Springfield

- Celebration by Kool and the Gang

- I Love a Rainy Night by Eddie Rabbitt

- 9 to 5 by Dolly Parton

- Angel of the Morning by Juice Newton

- America by Neil Diamond

- Another Brick in the Wall by Pink Floyd

- It's Still Rock 'N' Roll to Me by Billy Joel

- Lost In Love by Air Supply

- Ride like the Wind by Christopher Cross

- Sailing by Christopher Cross

- Against the Wind by Bob Seger and the Silver Bullet Band

- All Out of Love by Air Supply

- Fame by Irene Cara

- You May Be Right by Billy Joel

Song associated with leaving the Navy:

- Theme from the Greatest American Hero (Believe It or Not) by Joey Scarbury

  "Look at what's happened to me, I can't believe it myself.

  Suddenly, I am up on top of the world, it should've been somebody else.

  Believe it or not, I'm walking on air. I never thought I could feel so free.

  Flying away on a wing and a prayer. Who could it be?

  Believe it or not. It's just me."

Note to Grandchildren:

In living your life, try to focus on enjoying the journey. If your only happiness comes from reaching a specific destination, I'm afraid you are going to be very disappointed. In addition to this book, use my world travel experiences as an analogy. I've visited over 32 countries, and none of the destinations was what I expected. Some were nicer, some were worse, all were surprising, in some way. I try to enjoy the journey, regardless.

Finally, on your journey to "Mars," ignore the naysayers, along the way. Remember, "Living well is the best revenge."

Dear Reader, please leave a book review on Amazon.com or the platform where you purchased the book. I will read them all. Thanks again for joining me on this journey.

Jerry "Disco" Werner.

www.ingramcontent.com/pod-product-compliance
Lightning Source LLC
Chambersburg PA
CBHW042056150726
48005CB00032B/1080